The Art of **SERIES**
EDITED BY CHARLES BAXTER

The Art of series is a line of books reinvigorating the practice of craft and criticism. Each book is a brief, witty, and useful exploration of fiction, nonfiction, or poetry by a writer impassioned by a singular craft issue. *The Art of* volumes provide a series of sustained examinations of key, but sometimes neglected, aspects of creative writing by some of contemporary literature's finest practitioners.

The Art of Intimacy: The Space Between
by Stacey D'Erasmo

The Art of Description: World into Word by Mark Doty

The Art of the Poetic Line by James Longenbach

The Art of Daring: Risk, Restlessness, Imagination
by Carl Phillips

The Art of Attention: A Poet's Eye by Donald Revell

The Art of Time in Fiction: As Long As It Takes
by Joan Silber

The Art of Syntax: Rhythm of Thought, Rhythm of Song
by Ellen Bryant Voigt

*The Art of Recklessness: Poetry as Assertive Force and
Contradiction* by Dean Young

THE ART OF

PERSPECTIVE

WHO TELLS THE STORY

Other Books by Christopher Castellani

The Art of

PERSPECTIVE

WHO TELLS THE STORY

Christopher Castellani

Graywolf Press

This publication is made possible, in part, by the voters of Minnesota through a Minnesota State Arts Board Operating Support grant, thanks to a legislative appropriation from the arts and cultural heritage fund, and through a grant from the Wells Fargo Foundation Minnesota. Significant support has also been provided by Target, the McKnight Foundation, the Amazon Literary Partnership, and other generous contributions from foundations, corporations, and individuals. To these organizations and individuals we offer our heartfelt thanks.

Published by Graywolf Press
212 Third Avenue North, Suite 485
Minneapolis, Minnesota 55401

www.graywolfpress.org

Published in the United States of America

ISBN 978-1-55597-726-9

4 6 8 10 11 9 7 5

Library of Congress Control Number: 2015952174

Cover design: Scott Sorenson

for Michael

Each of us narrates our life as it suits us.

—Elena Ferrante

Contents

THE ART OF

PERSPECTIVE

WHO TELLS THE STORY

Introduction: *To Seeing Each Other Again*

I want to tell you what happened on the way to dinner. My husband and I were walking down Thirteenth Street in Philadelphia toward an upscale Italian BYOB. In one hand I carried a decent bottle of wine, in the other, my phone, to check directions. We both wore jackets and ties. Michael's shoes were new and, in my opinion, overpriced, but I didn't want to pick a fight. This was an arrivederci dinner. The next morning, Michael would fly home to Boston, and I would stay on in the Philly area to teach for the semester.

Though we'd spent months apart in the past, this time felt different. Middle age was messing with our heads. In the past few years, as if on cue, too many of our loved ones had divorced, or fallen seriously ill, or died. As lives went haywire around us, we'd come to regard each other's physical presence with a kind of wonder, dazzled by our very solidness. Just a week before, Michael had wept at our dining room table after finishing James Salter's *Light Years.*

I want so badly for you to know how it felt to walk beside him at that moment, in all its unrepeatable particularity. It matters that it was the Sunday of Labor Day weekend, a night of familiar wistfulness and languor and rapidly knotting anxiety; that the air was steamy but the sidewalks cool from a sudden afternoon rain; that most of the city was still down the shore (as one says in the region), which added to the sense of emptiness; that Michael and I had been together exactly fourteen years, one month, and three days; that even though we were in Philly's so-called Gayborhood, with rainbows painted onto the street signs, we were still too nervous to hold hands; and that, as we crossed Locust, a woman approached us.

"Can I walk with youse guys?" she asked, though she was already matching us step for step. "Pretend like we're together?"

We looked at each other. "Um, sure."

She seemed, in a word, crazy. She had a weathered, scarred face, blond hair stringy and frizzed, and the worn-down upper teeth of a druggie. She wore jeans, a yellow windbreaker, and torn-up sneakers. "Everybody on this street hates me," she said, clutching the multiple plastic bags she carried in both hands. "Thirteenth Street. This whole fucking neighborhood. I'm scared to walk by myself. You're my guardian angels."

She kept up with us, talking nonstop, inching closer as we veered away. We weren't afraid of her, exactly, but the streets were unlit, and the buildings closed, and, by any objective assessment, this was a troubled person. Where was she headed? Would she make a scene in front of the restaurant? Demand money? Offer sex? Would she ruin our last night together?

"I blew my brains out on cocaine in the '70s," she said, and then, with girlish buoyancy, she went on to describe the limitless freedom of that now-distant age, the wild parties that lasted into mornings, the friends who lived in the brownstones that surrounded us. All of these friends—mostly gay men, she made clear, some of whom were her lovers—were dead now. Those who were left were out to get her. They had a score to settle, though she never made its terms clear. Looking at the dark brownstones with alternating fondness and disgust, she said, "Nothing's like it used to be."

Whose story is this now? I thought I was telling it, that it was mine. Mine and Michael's. But this woman hijacked it. A block before the restaurant, she dashed off unannounced down an alley toward a lit-up church that might have been a mission. She never told us her name. Maybe it's her story. Or maybe this isn't a story at all, but an incident. A tangent. A few lines in a journal. And yet it's stayed with me. What, if anything, is it actually about?

Every student of fiction writing has been taught E. M. Forster's distinction between story and plot. In Forster's formulation, a story is a sequence of events linked merely by chronology: two men walk down a street, and then a paranoid woman walks with them for a while, and then the two men have dinner, and then the next day they say a poignant good-bye. In this story, you can rearrange the events and nothing truly essential will change. A plot, on the other hand, is a sequence of events whose relationship to each other is determined by causality: two men walk down a street, and because they remind her of men she once knew, a paranoid woman chooses them to walk with for a while for safety; shaken by the encounter in ways he can't quite express, one man begs the other over dinner not to fly home to Boston the next day; the other man promises to stay, but then, the next day, leaves anyway.

Of course, neither of these tales qualifies as riveting, but the latter is inarguably more interesting and less arbitrary than the former. Causality has given it meaning and context, what another essential writing teacher, Vivian Gornick, calls the *situation*. To confuse matters, Gornick makes the distinction between a situation and her own definition of *story*, which is different from Forster's. According to Gornick, the story is "the emotional experience that preoccupies the writer: the insight, the wisdom, the thing one has come to say." So, here, the situation is a late summer night in Philly, where two lovers are about to part; and the story is—well, I don't know the story yet.

I don't know because I haven't decided who's telling it. Let's say I want to turn this night in Philadelphia into a real story, either as fiction or as a personal essay. Like most writers, I'm ambitious; I want the story to be about *everything;* I want it to hold the deepest insights, to resonate far and wide, all while keeping readers eagerly turning the pages. I want it to be greater than the sum of its parts. I start building it in my head, paragraph by paragraph, and already I'm impatient for a more dynamic plot, for the histories and futures of the three characters I've been handed and for the connections among them. As I draft, I observe a hundred details I haven't even put down yet, and I'm formulating a theme, a Big Idea, something about gentrification, or youth, or AIDS, or the endurance of love, or—better yet!—all of the above. Then I get to thinking this could be a thriller, because who's to say that, on our way to the airport, we didn't hear on the radio that the body of a blond woman in a yellow windbreaker was found in an alley off Broad Street, and that the police are seeking any and all leads? Actually, I'm thinking I'm not even me anymore, that I'd be much more interesting as the woman's former lover, one of her men she thought was dead. She walks into the mission and there I am, and it's sweet at first, poignant, and then we get high, and then I kill her, and it's an accident but that's not how it looks, and then . . .

Stories are easy. We're all sitting on park benches with loaves of bread, stories coming at us like pigeons.

We're as hungry for the stories as the stories are to be told. We want to cram as many of them as we can onto every page, where they jostle with each other and with our Big Ideas for them. Ultimately, though, someone has to take charge, and that person must be the narrator, whether that's "me," "Michael," "the woman" (oh, let's just call her Charlene), her resurrected lover, another of her enemies, some other player, or an overarching entity—an omniscience—who manipulates us all. There is no more important decision the writer makes than who tells the story, because, whoever that narrator is, he will compel us to tell it his way, with his frames of reference, his agenda and lexicon and baggage, within his particular wedge of time.

Every narrator becomes the story, and the story becomes him. It is only and always his. This is what we mean when we say that the story is from "Christopher's perspective." We mean that what "really happened" to the other characters, especially but not exclusively in fiction, is Christopher's unique construction, filtered and shaped by his experience, sensibility, and facility with language and insight. We know them, and what happens to them, and how they felt about it, and what it "means," and the weather that day, and the relative value of his husband's shoes, only the way he knows them and how he wants us to know them, and *because* he wants us to know them, not necessarily because that is how they objectively *are.* In the process, Christopher-as-narrator constructs and reveals himself. There is no purity, no essential reliability. There is only the coherence of the narrator's vision for the tale he wants to tell, and the success or failure of his strategy for telling it.

Narration is perspective in action. It is the "delivering" of perspective to the reader or listener. That delivery system bears the unique stamp of the narrator's sensibility and his motley set of biases and agendas at the moment of telling. This makes every story, at its core, an *assertion* of perspective, with the narrator as the story's prime mover.

In itself, the word *perspective* has a static feel to it, and a kind of narrowness. One imagines a fixed point in the distance, a line of unbroken sight. A bowl of fruit on a table, maybe, rendered as a shapely still life. Similarly, the word *perspective* also connotes a strong personal conviction: "From my perspective," we hear the guy next door say, "vinyl siding should be banned in this neighborhood." In most cases, in both a painting and a conversation, we can replace "perspective" with "the way I see it"; and, by definition, that way of seeing is always limited by its identification with a single person, the artist or the speaker. In my formulation of perspective's relationship to storytelling, perspective is more dynamic and more ample. It acts like a vector, in that it has direction as well as magnitude. In other words, perspective carries the weight of the narrator who delivers it. It contains his multitudes and contradictions. In a story, life can never be still. It must vibrate. The fruit rots in the bowl. A snake writhes among the apples. The table overturns. And it all happens in just the way the narrator sees it happen.

Author and narrator collaborate in the telling of a story, but it is impossible to quantify how much the two share. In their act of collaboration, they are in a continual state of merging and diverging, identification and resistance. As hard as an author tries, she can never fully become her narrator, nor can she ever fully separate herself from her. In this way, the act of writing a story or personal essay is a process of occupying two states of being simultaneously, of seeing a world both the way your narrator sees it and, try as you might to resist it, the way you see it. It's no wonder so many narrators seem like thinly veiled versions of the authors themselves, and not just when they're of similar age, gender, politics, or circumstance; unable to escape her own sensibility, the author inevitably watches helplessly as it shines through in the words and thoughts of her narrator, a woman who, on the surface, may appear nothing like her.

There's no need for a veil in a personal essay, but I've already decided that my encounter with Charlene is not interesting enough for one of those. I'm not much of a memoirist, anyway, for all that sticking to the so-called truth; I feel claustrophobic, trapped in a little brain with that narrator-who's-also-me. I want this real-life encounter to be the raw material for a piece of fiction, probably a short story but maybe a novella. (Who knows? It's early.) We write what we know, even when that's not our intention. We can't help but reveal ourselves to ourselves. My original impulse to tell you about my night in Philly was significant enough that, at some point during dinner, I tapped a few of the details into my phone. My impulse was—and still is—to understand its implication, and for you to feel something; but what is the implication, and what do I want you to feel about it? How will I get you to feel it? Most importantly, who's going to take charge and be my narrator, and what will his or her strategy be?

Let me get back to you.

In the meantime, I want to understand better how to tell good stories, mostly so I can keep the reader or the listener in the room. (Don't we just love an audience? Don't I love that you've stuck with this little book so far, that every leap from word to word, sentence to sentence, has been and will continue to be an act of faith on your part?) I want to understand why one narrator compels us and another—maybe even one with a better story—leaves us cold. I believe in the potential for chemistry between any reader and character, and I believe in the irrational and inconsistent subjectivities of taste, but I believe most strongly in an author's artful and intentional manipulations. In other words, I believe in craft, which is nothing more than an informed bet an author makes on the set of tools at her disposal.

Narration is craft's most powerful, defining, and revealing tool. If there are such things as answers or secrets when it comes to how to tell good stories, they have already been told to us by the narrators of the novels and stories that have charged and changed us. Have we been paying attention?

Toward a Narrative Strategy

One may as well begin with that gossipy fellow who narrates *Howards End*.

"One may as well begin with Helen's letters to her sister," he[1] says, and with these opening lines Forster introduces both the Schlegel sisters and the anonymous voice that will deliver the narrator's perspective and bring the sisters and every other character alive for the reader. He seems rather nonchalant in that first sentence—why *not* begin with Helen's letters? It's as arbitrary a place as any—not to mention mildly exasperated and even a bit daunted by the task ahead. He's then generous (or lazy?) enough to allow the letters themselves, unfiltered and unabridged, to take up the rest of chapter 1. In the letters, Helen summarizes her visit with the Wilcox family at their country

---

1. Let's just say "he," though the narrator's gender is never definitively identified, despite a few literary critics' arguments to the contrary. The narrator is neither "Forster" nor the speaker who refers to women as "us" at the end of chapter 28. To argue the former is too reductive; to argue the latter is a stretch, given that the speaker in that scene could just as likely be Margaret herself.

home—the enchanting wych-elm, the dog-roses, the hay fever—and, in the final installment, confesses her love for Paul Wilcox, "the younger son who only came here Wednesday."

The present action really starts in chapter 2, in the scene at the breakfast table. Helen's sister, Margaret, sits with their aunt Juley, fretting over Helen's impetuous behavior, which the reader intuits will have wide-reaching implications. The scene is all dialogue, as if in a play, until, midconversation, the narrator reappears to describe the Schlegels' Wickham Place home, which is separated from the main road by a large promontory thickly settled with large, expensive flats, so that "one had the sense of a backwater, or rather of an estuary, whose waters flowed in from the invisible sea," creating "a certain measure of peace." Older houses like the Schlegels' "would be swept away in time," the narrator tells us, "and another promontory would rise upon their site, as humanity piled itself higher and higher on the precious soil of London."

Gone, already, are the nonchalance and objectivity of that first line. In their place: an attitude. It's this attitude—somewhat arch, more than a little fussy, frequently wise—that will infuse the narration for the rest of the novel and become the reader's delightful companion, eager to dish on everything from the love lives of the Schlegels and Wilcoxes to the evolving demographics of London to the nature of life itself. We readers imagine this guy continually pulling us close, whispering color commentary in our ears, shaping the experience in ways beyond the characters' abilities or intentions. "I hope that it will not set the reader against her," he whispers to us at the end of chapter 2, then proceeds to share that, to Margaret, "the [train] station of King's Cross had always suggested Infinity," and that its twin arches "were fit portals for some eternal adventure, whose issue might be prosperous, but would certainly not be expressed in the ordinary language of prosperity." Such a flight of fancy is rare for the otherwise grounded Margaret—the "sense" to Helen's "sensibility"—and in case we start to find her just as daft as her sister, our narrator jumps in to rescue her: "If you think this ridiculous," he says, "remember that it is not Margaret who is telling you about it; and let me hasten to add that they were in plenty of time for the train."

Addressing the reader directly, or even the narrator's awareness of the reading audience, is not a groundbreaking or even uncommon move, of course, even in 1910. It's already been sixty-three years since Jane Eyre kept turning to us throughout her tale of woe, most famously to say, "Reader, I married him." The difference in *Howards End* is that it's not a character— main or minor—who addresses us, but the unnamed and unbodied narrator. "Remember that it is not Margaret who is telling you about it," he says; okay, but who *is*? Can we trust him?

Fiction writers are taught that the first pages of a novel or story serve as a contract that highly subjective readers will either accept or reject. When we cast a novel aside early on, it's because we find something unappealing about the terms of that contract. We're not engaged by the voice, or the plot takes too long to rev up, or the main character doesn't compel us, or the language is too plain or poetic or pretentious, or magical realism just isn't our bag; the list of reasons for abandoning a book, during or after its opening salvo, could fill a book of its own. But what is this so-called contract with the reader but the author's attempt to establish her *narrative strategy,* and what is a reader's acceptance or rejection of the contract if not the acceptance or rejection of the strategy overall?

By narrative strategy, I mean the set of organizing principles that (in)form how the author is telling the story. If perspective is a way of seeing, and narration is perspective in action, then a narrative strategy is the how and the why of that seeing.

Just as every driver has some idea how to get from one destination to the next and a rationale for having chosen her route, every story has a narrative strategy.

However, not every driver chooses the most efficient route, even when her goal is to get to her destination quickly; nor does she always choose the most scenic route, even when her goal is to enjoy the views along the way. Similarly, not every writer chooses the most effective narrative strategy to achieve the effects she wants to have on the reader; most importantly, she often doesn't understand how certain craft choices contribute to or diminish that desired effect. Readers may not register these craft choices by name, but they sense when they are off: when, for example, the narrator knows too much or not enough; or when the omniscience feels out of proportion and the level of detail too specific or too broad; or when a story needs the wisdom of retrospection from a character stuck stubbornly and myopically in the present action.

Point of view is at its core, but a narrative strategy is not simply whether a narrator in a work of fiction uses "I," "you," "s/he," or, as go the trends, "we." It is not just whether the story's told in past or present, or whether there are quotation marks around what the characters say out loud, or even how many consciousnesses the narrator occupies. It's all of these and more. It's the unique philosophy behind the construction of a work of fiction that applies to that work alone. It's the type of narrator, limited by age and education and experience, speaking from a particular point in time. It's the degree of retrospection, and her level of diction, and the presence or absence of footnotes; it's a choice as seemingly small as whether or not to stick a name under the chapter heading or let the reader figure out who's narrating. The narrative strategy doesn't determine every choice an author makes in a work, but every choice an author makes must answer to the narrative strategy. Its greatest virtues are consistency and internal resonance; its archenemy is the arbitrary.

The mockumentary style of the American television show *The Office* is a big part of its narrative strategy. So is Ron Howard's disembodied voice, which introduces and interrupts each episode of *Arrested Development.* So are the letters to God that make up virtually all of Alice Walker's *The Color Purple,* and so is the obsessive detailing of Part One of Ian McEwan's *Atonement.* The mockumentary, the voice-over, the epistolary structure, the obsessive detailing: each of these is a necessary "how" that points to a "why," and each helps to deliver the storyteller's perspective. The "why" of *The Office*'s mockumentary style is that it essentially spoofs reality television, just as Ron Howard's voice of reason is a necessary counterpoint to the pathologically deluded Bluth family. Celie's letters to God act as literal manifestations of her quest for connection, recognition, and validation, just as Briony's chapters act as literal manifestations of both her guilt and her desire to re-create her family's lost world precisely as it was, down to the candlestick. These are examples of narrative strategies that mostly "work," but in no way am I suggesting that they were the only or even the most effective narrative strategies for these texts. Numerous possibilities were available to the creators and authors, of course, and we'll never know whether, in the final analysis, the mockumentary frame was too forced, or the voice-over needlessly intrusive, or the epistolary form too limiting, or if the preponderance of detail slowed too much of the momentum. Unless it's a text as extraordinary as the facsimile edition of T. S. Eliot's *The Waste Land,* in which Ezra Pound's edits overlay the original in a palimpsest and serve as a kind of second narrator, the book we pick up is the final product and nothing more. The vestiges of other potential strategies, other narrative options, do not haunt anyone but the author.

A veteran editor of a publishing house once told me that, even though novels have always been her first love as a reader, she prefers to work on book-length nonfiction as an editor. A book of nonfiction blooms with research, she said; it gets deeper and more convincing as it comes into its own. By contrast, the process of editing a novel draft or a book of stories, especially in the negotiation with the author, is often one of patching up, adding material, and stitching it all together. The magic she felt upon receiving the original version from the author seeps out with every draft, and all she can see are the seams. Or, to use another metaphor, the organic book she bought suddenly tastes processed. I think this is part of the reason most fiction writers feel like frauds: we know firsthand how little magic went into the revision process, how easily we forced our characters to go a different way from the way we originally imagined, how ruthlessly we cut and shape-shifted in order to suit the overall project and to achieve consistency and effect. As important as our narrators are, we are shockingly disloyal to them. When we need them to take a different perspective, and when we need a different strategy or to better accommodate the one we've settled on, we throw them to the wolves.

When last we left *Howards End*, we were just beginning to grasp the terms of its narrative strategy. We were still, as it were, going over the contract. It takes a little while, especially in a novel. Though first lines make a statement, and first chapters give a strong sense of the author's design, neither is determinative. We need a more generous sample of pages; we need to be a bit farther down the road toward our destination.

"Remember that it is not Margaret who is telling you about it," we read on page twelve, but, of course, as

Howards End continues, we don't remember that at all. The primary reason for this is that Forster makes extensive use of free indirect style, that mode in which the narrator continually fuses with various characters one at a time, inhabiting their consciousnesses, and, in showing us the world through their eyes, disappears into them. These character (in)fusions last for a few pages or for just a moment before the narrator reappears as himself or jumps into the head of another character. Though the narrator of *Howards End* appears to mind-jump indiscriminately, before long it becomes clear that he prefers Margaret's and Helen's minds over all the others. In fact, the most significant index of the Schlegel sisters' privilege in the novel is the narrator's choice to give himself over to them so many times, cede the stage to them, and thereby grant them the space and time to tell so much of their stories in their own words, both in dialogue and in internal monologue. It's a form of respect as much as it is good storytelling: if our narrator and guide, the one we're trusting to organize the story for us, finds Margaret and Helen so compelling, then maybe we should, too. This is especially true when we consider how many readers view the narrator as a stand-in for the author. *Respect* might sound like a strange word in this context, but I think it's an appropriate gauge for the relationship between any narrator and his characters and between any narrator and his readers.

Forster sends many such signals in the first four chapters of *Howards End,* but it's not until chapter 5 that his narrative strategy solidifies, and that the perspective becomes clear. It's the first chapter in what might be called the second movement of the novel and takes place after "the Wilcox episode," the main thrust of the first movement and the subject of that set of letters from Helen to her sister, "[falls] into the background."

Chapter 5 begins with a hyperbolic pronouncement from our narrator, the haughty attitude we glimpsed in chapter 2 now in full flower: "It will be generally admitted," he says, "that Beethoven's Fifth Symphony is the most sublime noise that has ever penetrated into the ear of man. All sorts and conditions are satisfied by it." He then proceeds to mind-jump among all the characters gathered in the Queen's Hall to hear that sublime noise:

> Whether you are like Mrs. Munt, and tap surreptitiously when the tunes come—of course, not so as to disturb the others; or like Helen, who can see heroes and shipwrecks in the music's flood; or like Margaret, who can only see the music; or like Tibby, who is profoundly versed in counterpoint, and holds the full score open on his knee; or like their cousin, Fräulein Mosebach, who remembers all the time that Beethoven is "echt Deutsch"; or like Fräulein

Mosebach's young man, who can remember nothing but Fräulein Mosebach: in any case, the passion of your life becomes more vivid, and you are bound to admit that such a noise is cheap at two shillings. It is cheap, even if you hear it in the Queen's Hall, dreariest music-room in London, though not as dreary as the Free Trade Hall, Manchester; and even if you sit on the extreme left of that hall, so that the brass bumps at you before the rest of the orchestra arrives, it is still cheap.

He's showing off a bit here, flexing his narrator muscles, all the while demonstrating the flexibility of free indirect discourse. More importantly, he's continuing the process of marking his territory, a process that began with the first sentence. For the past four chapters, he's been telling us not only what he knows, but what he *can* know. Here in chapter 5, he's reminding us that he has access to what every character is thinking at any given moment. He knows music, too, and the London music scene well enough to tell you where the best seats are in which houses, and at what price. He's also got some thoughts on the passion of life, or lack thereof.

One of the great pleasures and frustrations with *Howards End*'s narrative strategy—and with free indirect discourse in general—is that the reader is often unsure whether a character's thoughts or internal monologue belong solely to herself or to the narrator who has fused with her. Sometimes it's both, sometimes it's one, and sometimes it's the other. Context matters, but context doesn't always offer a satisfying answer. Does Margaret know she can "only see the music," or is that the narrator characterizing her as the "sensible" sister? Does Helen really see heroes and shipwrecks, or is that the narrator's interpretation of what the "romantic" sister is seeing? In most cases, the narrator can have it both ways, but when he doesn't, he attempts to clarify who's thinking what, as in the first line of the next long paragraph of chapter 5:

> For the Andante had begun—very beautiful, but bearing a family likeness to all the other beautiful Andantes that Beethoven had written, and, to Helen's mind, rather disconnecting the heroes and shipwrecks of the first movement from the heroes and goblins of the third.

It's a workmanlike sentence that most readers gloss over, but look closer and it's also a nifty little demonstration of craft that shows the narrator's control. We know we're in his head for the first half of the sentence because we recognize his voice; it's the same one that declared Beethoven's Fifth Symphony "the most sublime noise that has ever penetrated into the ear of man." But then, midway through, the sentence pivots on the phrase "to Helen's mind." These three seemingly innocuous words are an example of what John Gardner famously called "needless filtering . . . through some observing consciousness." According to Gardner, a narrator need not observe that a character is thinking something; in fact, Gardner views the inclusion of such an observation as the mark of the amateur writer. It's the amateur writer, then, who needlessly attaches phrases like "she thought," "she noticed," "it seemed to her that," "to Helen's mind," and the like to his character's internal thoughts and descriptions. In this case, though, Forster—not an amateur, it's safe to say—wants to make the reader keenly aware that the second half of this sentence belongs not to the narrator alone, but firmly to Helen, or, at least, to both Helen and the narrator in their fused state. The phrase "to Helen's mind" is itself a directional signal from the narrator indicating the fusion that's about to occur between the comma and the word *rather.* As Gardner taught, though, this sort of directional signal shouldn't be necessary; so why is it necessary here?

It's probably *not* necessary, but it does do important work. It's one perfectly legitimate way for the narrator to eliminate ambiguity from a scene in which ambiguity is not productive. You see, what's about to happen in this scene at the Queen's Hall will change the course of Helen's life forever, and so it's crucial to Forster's narrative strategy that the reader both understand Helen's unique vision of the world and emotionally invest in her—connect *and* cathect[2] with her, if you will—in the next nine paragraphs, that period of time between the beginning of the andante and when she flees for home with the wrong umbrella.

There is no mind-jumping in this interlude; the nine paragraphs belong unquestionably to Helen. Throughout, the narrator makes much use of filtering consciousness to reinforce that we are seeing the world through Helen's eyes as she muses nonchalantly about how "interesting" her "row of people was." "What diverse influences had gone to the making!" she thinks. Then the music changes, and the "terrible" goblins of the first movement reappear, and Helen "[observes] in passing that there [is] no such thing as splendour or heroism in the world." The moment, seemingly so benign, shakes her:

---

2. Why don't we use this word—*cathect*—more often? It means "to invest with mental or emotional energy." It's better than "to root for," in that it implies an identification with a character, a throwing in of a lot with her. You can't cathect with her from the sidelines; her heart beats along with yours. But, as we'll see later, it doesn't necessarily mean you *like* her.

After the interlude of elephants dancing, [the goblins] returned and made the observation for the second time. Helen could not contradict them, for, once at all events, she had felt the same, and had seen the reliable walls of youth collapse. Panic and emptiness! Panic and emptiness! The goblins were right.

The phrase "panic and emptiness," introduced here for the first time, is a leitmotif in the novel that comes to define Helen. It is important not only because of its uniqueness to Helen, though, but also because it embodies Forster's own anxieties about the imminent blurriness of the class, of city and country, of the order into which he was born. In this defining scene, Helen's metaphor expands and intensifies into what is essentially an apocalyptic vision of the world, one in which the goblins remain a constant threat even after they're no longer visible:

They might return—and they did. It was as if the splendour of life might boil over and waste to steam and froth. In its dissolution one heard the terrible, ominous note, and a goblin, with increased malignity, walked quietly over the universe from end to end. Panic and emptiness! Panic and emptiness! Even the flaming ramparts of the world might fall.

Beethoven chose to make all right in the end. . . .

He brought back the gusts of splendour, the heroism, the youth, the magnificence of life and of death,
and, amid vast roarings of a superhuman joy, he led
his Fifth Symphony to its conclusion. But the goblins
were there. They could return.

In the midst of this emotional spiral, Helen flees for
home, mistakenly taking Leonard Bast's ratty umbrella,
an act that sets off the chain of events that will result
in both her shame and her victory over the Wilcoxes.
"The music summed up to her all that had happened or
could happen in her career," she thinks as she leaves the
Queen's Hall, and she's right. Though *Howards End* offers an ostensibly happy ending, it's an ending suffused
with the same anxiety that makes its first and most
memorable appearance in Helen's mind at the Queen's
Hall on this fateful afternoon at the start of chapter 5.
"London's creeping," Helen says, many years later, at
the novel's close, as she points her finger over "eight or
nine meadows, but at the end of them was a red rust."
Moments later, she completes the thought by telling
Margaret, "And London is only part of something else,
I'm afraid. Life's going to be melted down, all over the
world."

It is Forster's use of free indirect style—the centerpiece
of his narrative strategy—that gives the foundational

scene at the Queen's Hall a power strong and memorable enough to resonate at the end of the novel. Yes, the images are vivid in both, and the emotions high, but images and emotion aren't enough. Stories filled with great images and intense emotion are, at this moment, falling flat all over the world. To understand how free indirect style helps these scenes succeed, how it helps whoever tells the story to tell it more effectively, it's useful to go back to the difference between free indirect style and filtered consciousness.

John Gardner's reason for admonishing the writer not to use filtering consciousness is because it makes for less "vivid" prose; he also implies, rightly, the redundancy of such phrases as "she noticed" and "she saw." But the most dramatic effect filtering consciousness has in fiction is that it creates *distance* between character and reader, a distance occupied by the needlessly explanatory narrator. Here's the example Gardner himself gives us in *The Art of Fiction:*

> The amateur writes: "Turning, she noticed two snakes fighting in among the rocks." Compare: "She turned. In among the rocks, two snakes were fighting."

It's true that the second example is more vivid and less redundant. But more important, and more crucial when it comes to the success of a novel like *Howards*

End and any novel written in third person, is the *intimacy* created in the moment between the sentence "She turned" and the one that begins "In among the rocks." In that white space between the period and the word *In* the reader subconsciously *becomes* the character, whoever that "she" may be. We become the ones doing the noticing, albeit through her eyes. It's an immediate identification, a fusion much like the one Forster's narrator enacts with multiple characters throughout *Howards End.* Again, the reader doesn't consciously register this intimacy; it is achieved by the lack of narrative obstruction.

Through this same lens, consider another harmless little sentence, plucked from one of those nine paragraphs in chapter 5 when Helen's mind begins to wander after the andante:

And next to her was Aunt Juley, so British, and wanting to tap.

That same intimacy happens between the words "Aunt Juley" and "so British."

We become Helen, thinking, in her own somewhat droll and petulant voice, "so British." As in Gardner's example, no narrator interrupts the reader here to tell us what the character is "noticing" or "thinking." We forget for a moment that there is a narrator at all. He has done the work to get us alone in the audience with Helen, aligned with her; that alignment—that shrinking of narrative distance to the point of eclipse—helps us to understand her, to connect and cathect with her. By the time the goblins return at the end of the nine paragraphs, we are experiencing the scene *as Helen*. We're alone with her and the goblins, feeling the panic and emptiness along with her, which is the primary reason the images and emotion affect us at all and then stick with us. Forster employs filtering consciousness to make sure we know we are in Helen's mind; but once he gets us there, that redundant and distance-creating scaffolding becomes unnecessary.

There is an inherent intimacy that comes prepackaged with first-person narration, even when, as in *Howards End*, the narrator is nameless and omniscient. In general, a reader can't help but feel a closeness with anyone who refers to herself as "I" and tells us a story. There is something deceptively organic about the exchange, as if the words on the page hadn't been written or constructed. That very same narrator in third person seems to speak to us from a remove; we are conscious that a third party, off in some attic somewhere, has fashioned her, attached those quotation marks and commas and "she saids" to her speech, and shaped her thoughts into sentences she wouldn't or couldn't think of without the help of someone with a better vocabulary and time on his hands. The more help this character needs—the further the narrative voice from her own frames of reference, lexicon, and level of insight—the further away the reader perceives her to be. And when filtering consciousness is used, an even greater distance is created.

Free indirect style has the effect of eclipsing the psychic distance between reader and character, and between reader and narrator, because it borrows the "voicey" and "organic" qualities of first person and integrates them into third. While I may have just overstated my case when I argued that the reader *becomes* Helen in this sentence—

> And next to her was Aunt Juley, so British, and wanting to tap.

—it is no overstatement that the reader is closer to Helen because of the very Helen-ness of those two little words, *so British.* Consider this exaggerated rewrite, meant to deliberately increase the psychic distance:

> And next to her was Aunt Juley, who'd always struck Helen as quintessentially British, and wanting to tap.

The diction here is appropriate to Helen's age and education, but obviously the intimacy has been lost.

There is nothing "wrong" with the sentence as long as it's the author's intention to create or maintain a certain level of distance between reader and character. In some cases, as we'll see in Forster's later novel *A Passage to India*, distance is not only desired but necessary.

I want to return, briefly, to the question of trusting the narrator. If, God help us, we were critiquing Forster's manuscript in a creative writing workshop, by now someone would have brought up the possibility that our gossipy fellow is *unreliable.* We were all taught this term in high school, where it was applied to demonstrably demented speakers or those with skewed perceptions of reality: Whitey in Ring Lardner's "Haircut," the speaker of Denis Johnson's "Emergency," and, perhaps most famously, Vladimir Nabokov's Humbert Humbert. These characters almost always speak in an idiosyncratic first-person voice, unmistakable and memorable for not only the content of what they are saying but also how they are saying it. The great pleasure here is in the dramatic irony that such speakers offer us, and in the privileged position in which it puts us; we are allowed to know the character better than he knows himself and even to pass judgment on him if it suited us. Back then, the speaker had to be pretty misguided to get slapped with the "unreliable" label, and, once his misguidedness became clear, it became the *point* of the story. These often got billed as character studies, which is something of a euphemism for stories in which the main character's take on the plot that unfolds around him is more compelling than the plot itself.

The term *unreliable narrator,* coined in 1961, has been retroactively and promiscuously applied to speakers from the Greeks to the postmodernists. In the meantime, it's also become a staple of writing workshops, embedded in the question of who tells the story. Frequently the class zooms in on it as the locus of the "problem," and much time is spent deciding whether the author should either amp up the crazy or remove all traces of it. The former is meant to fix a weak voice or compensate for a less than dynamic plot, the latter to inspire confidence in the character and, transitively, the author. "Use it or lose it," I can hear myself saying to the silent author dutifully transcribing our conversation. It's never so simple, but it's a start. Reevaluating the narrative voice through the lens of reliability invariably forces the writer to confront a wide range of choices, from character motivation to the degree of retrospection.

Lately, though, I've noticed that the "unreliable narrator" label is being applied not only to the obviously deluded first-person speaker, but also to the third-person narrator who exhibits even a smidgen of a personality.

An attitude, if you will. We are particularly alert to, and made slightly uneasy by, any narrator who reveals an attitude, especially if that narrator is unidentified. We are uncomfortable enough with his authority to slap him with the "unreliable" label. Implicit in this is the recognition, however subconscious, that all stories are constructed, and that the person telling the story always brings to it his biases and sensibility and unique take. That just because a narrator isn't demonstrably crazy doesn't mean that his interpretation of a series of events would match yours if you both had to recount them. That no two experiences are alike. That what makes every narrator essentially unreliable is the simple fact of his humanity.

An effective narrative strategy gives the narrator(s) maximum flexibility within well-defined and purposeful limits and constraints. Choosing those limits and constraints is among the most difficult decisions a writer makes when she first conceives of a story or novel. Though *Howards End* is technically told in an omniscient first-person point of view, the closer we look at it, the more clearly we can see that there are restrictions on what the narrator can know, on how much he is willing to share, on how he can share it, and from what point in time.

In showing us what he knows and can know, the

narrator also demarcates what he *can't* know. The music halls outside London, or in Paris, what of those? What of the people sitting next to the Schlegels at the Queen's Hall—what are *they* thinking, not only about the music, but about the Schlegels? The narrator can see and interpret quite clearly the present lives of the characters—at the breakfast table, waiting for a train, sitting in rows listening to Beethoven—but what about their futures? He doesn't seem to be privy to them, or, at the very least, isn't saying. Time and again, he establishes his ability to zoom across the present thoughts of all the characters in the moment, and fill in their various lineages and backstories as well, but not his ability to tell us what will become of them. In other words, he has located himself firmly a mere half step ahead of the present action, not from a point in time that would give him the benefit of retrospection. Not only does this build tension and increase suspense; also it enhances the feeling that the reader is experiencing the events of the novel alongside the narrator and characters.

Within these limits that Forster imposes on his narrator, he is wonderfully, thrillingly flexible, a shapeshifter, simultaneously himself and a host of characters, sometimes just Helen, sometimes just Margaret, and sometimes just himself, moving from present to past at will, signaling shifts in time and perspective when he needs to, and allowing other moments to remain productively ambiguous. In one of his more contemplative moments, at the end of the novel's second movement, he—or maybe it's he and Margaret; it's hard to be sure— tells us what this whole *Howards End* thing might be about after all, and why we might want to keep reading to see how it plays out:

> Actual life is full of false clues and sign-posts that lead nowhere. With infinite effort we nerve ourselves for a crisis that never comes. . . . The tragedy of preparedness has scarcely been handled, save by the Greeks. Life is indeed dangerous, but not in the way morality would have us believe. It is indeed unmanageable, but the essence of it is not a battle. It is unmanageable because it is a romance, and its essence is romantic beauty.

As concerns go, those of *Howards End* are limited to the relatively domestic and philosophical: romance, beauty, morality, love. It's a novel about the social and intellectual and romantic lives of middle-class Londoners during a specific period of historical time, when class distinctions are blurring simultaneously with those of the city and the country. The how of Forster's narrative strategy—the chatty guide a half step ahead of the action, the frequent fusion with the consciousness of two middle-class sisters in relationships with men of different classes, the deliberate balance of filtering consciousness with free indirect style—fits snugly with the why of these thematic concerns. The form is in harmony with the content, as it is in *The Office, Arrested Development, The Color Purple, Atonement.* One can't imagine such a text being told any other way, by anyone else.

A narrative strategy, however effective it may be in one work of fiction, is not transferable to another. If only it were that easy. If only each new novel or story didn't come with its own set of requirements, its own moods and vision. If only it could stretch to fit what worked so beautifully the last time. Faulkner could have stopped trying after *As I Lay Dying* and written all of his future books with that same mosaic structure. Rather than waste a bunch of time coming up with the pseudo-biographer who narrates *Orlando,* Woolf could have stuck with the omniscient stream-of-consciousness strategy of *Mrs. Dalloway* or, for that matter, *To the Lighthouse.*

The constraints of Forster's narrative strategy in *Howards End* would have choked his next published novel, *A Passage to India.* The intricate politics of colonial India; the (in)compatibility of East and West; the supposed sexual assault of a British woman by an Indian man in a remote, dark, echoing cave; race riots in the streets: this is far from the territory of the fellow who read us Helen's letters to her sister. His voice could not have accommodated it. To adequately guide us through such different territory requires not only a different narrator, but a more flexible and accommodating method of integrating contextual information. Somehow, the reader will need to be provided with the geography and culture and political landscape of British India so that we can grasp fully both the interpersonal drama among the main characters and the allegorical implications of that drama.

The long first paragraph of *A Passage to India*, a marked contrast to the casual opening of *Howards End*, sends an immediate signal that the scope, depth, and breadth of this book will be different:

Except for the Marabar Caves—and they are twenty miles off—the city of Chandrapore presents nothing extraordinary. Edged rather than washed by the river Ganges, it trails for a couple of miles along the bank, scarcely distinguishable from the rubbish it deposits so freely. . . . Chandrapore was never large or beautiful, but two hundred years ago it lay on the road between Upper India, then imperial, and the sea, and the fine houses date from that period. . . . The very wood seems made of mud, the inhabitants of mud moving. So abased, so monotonous is everything that meets the eye, that when the Ganges comes down it might be expected to wash the excrescence back into the soil. Houses do fall, people are drowned and left rotting, but the general outline of the town persists, swelling here, shrinking there, like some low but indestructible form of life.

The narrator goes on to describe the other features of the city: the hospital, the civil station, the English gardens. Then the personified sky, encompassing the clouds and stars and sun, which "settles everything." At the close of the chapter-long panorama, which has yet to include a single human character, there's this view of the vast landscape:

No mountains infringe on the curve. League after league the earth lies flat, heaves a little, is flat again. Only in the south, where a group of fists and fingers are thrust up through the soil, is the endless expanse interrupted. These fists and fingers are the Marabar Hills, containing the extraordinary caves.

Talk about distance! The perspective from which the narrator speaks in this chapter is literally from miles above. One imagines him[3] looking down from a seat in the heavens, not over from the next aisle at Queen's

---

3. From now on—in an attempt at clarity—I will assign any narrator whose gender is unspecified the gender of the author.

Hall on a rainy afternoon. But of course the distance is not just spatial. Godlike in his omniscience, he is apparently also unconstrained by time, with limitless access. If the opening chapters of every novel set its narrative terms and boundaries, these few paragraphs alone announce that no detail is outside the narrator's purview, that nothing can escape his eye. More importantly, his concerns—and, therefore, the concerns of the novel— don't appear, at least at first, to be personal; they are historical, maybe even biblical. It's worth noting that, in my edition, "Part I: Mosque" is printed above the heading to chapter 1; flipping ahead, one can see the book's three-part structure: Mosque, Caves, Temple. No, this story doesn't seem personal at all; it seems, from just this opening salvo, archetypal.

Like the narrator in *Howards End,* the godlike speaker we meet in chapter 1 of *A Passage to India* eventually fuses with various characters. There is a similar investment in free indirect style, in mind-jumping among a relatively large cast of characters. Here, too, the narrator has his favorites among the cast, who just so happen to represent West and East: Adela Quested, a British woman newly arrived in Chandrapore with her potential future mother-in-law, Mrs. Moore; and Dr. Aziz, a young Indian man who befriends Mrs. Moore after a chance encounter at the local mosque, and who is later accused of raping Adela in the Marabar Caves.

And yet even these privileged characters remain at a remove. One reason for this sense of remove is that, unlike *Howards End*, the novel is told in third person, without the intimacy of the "I" speaker accompanying the reader, but that reason alone is insufficient. It's as if the narrator can't or won't overcome the psychic distance he must travel in order to achieve fusion with any of the privileged characters; the effect, then, is less like fusion and more like a quick swooping-down. He rarely stays in one character's head for long before returning to his perch. It's from this perch that he can describe the Ganges, the heat, the hills; it's where he can transcribe the machinations of the various Chandrapore officials and explore the philosophy put forth by minor but significant figures like Professor Godbole; it's where he can muse, however uncomfortably for the modern audience, on the nature of the "Orientals" as compared to the British. There is a tonal sameness throughout the entire novel, even when the narrator ostensibly disappears into the heads of his privileged characters to see the world through their eyes. The narrator is ventriloquizing, but we can see his lips moving.

As a result, the main characters in *A Passage to India*, while credible and memorable and vivid, do not work their way into the reader's heart. The narrator takes Aziz and Adela, and to an extent Mrs. Moore and Cyril Fielding, on a personal emotional journey—a marriage plot, in fact—but it's the ideas and politics behind the journey that we remember, that stick with us. This is not necessarily a failure of empathy, but a matter of narrative priorities: setting them and adhering to them. We cathect with Aziz and Adela *just enough.* The book's success doesn't depend on whether we love or understand them; we just need to know who they are. What's much more important to the narrative strategy is that we know what they mean.

It's fitting, then, that *A Passage to India* begins so expansively on a characterless landscape and that, throughout, the narrator speeds through the rare moments of emotion and introspection that *Howards End* might embrace and explore. Take Dr. Aziz, just as the reader is getting to know him, on the anniversary of his wife's death:

And unlocking a drawer, he took out his wife's photograph. He gazed at it, and tears spouted from his eyes. He thought, "How unhappy I am!" But because he really was unhappy, another emotion soon mingled with his self-pity: he desired to remember his wife and could not. Why could he remember people whom he did not love? They were always so vivid to him, whereas the more he looked at this photograph, the less he saw. She had eluded him thus, ever since they had carried her to her tomb. He had known that she would pass from his hands and eyes, but had thought she could live in his mind, not realizing that the very fact that we have loved the dead increases

their unreality, and that the more passionately we
invoke them the further they recede.

The relative clunkiness, or at least the halfhearted-
ness, of this passage reveals that the narrator is out of
his comfort zone. It's not just that he's brought us a
scene in which a character picks up a photograph, cries
over it, and tells himself, almost cartoonishly, how unhappy he is. It's both how quickly the narrator takes
over afterward, and that he takes the opportunity to
explain the nature of grief in a way that Aziz cannot.
In going beyond the character's capacity for insight as
well as his tonal register, the narrator elevates himself,
positions himself as the authority on matters of life
and death, and thereby widens the distance between
Aziz and the reader. We sympathize with Aziz, but our
hearts aren't breaking. We sense (accurately, as it turns
out) that we have other things to focus on, and that the
narrator will get to them soon enough.

A similar, but even more striking, thing happens
on the day that Adela testifies in court against Aziz.
The mystery at the heart of the novel's plot—the chief
unknown—has been what happened between her and
Aziz in the Marabar cave, and finally Adela will be forced
to describe the incident and face cross-examination.
Not only must she have a lot on her mind, but the narrator must feel obligated to convey her emotional state,
both before and after her testimony. Instead, though,

he tells us that the first person Adela notices upon entering the courtroom is the punkah wallah, the "almost naked, and splendidly formed" man who "caught her attention" and "seemed to control the proceedings":

He had the strength and beauty that sometimes come to flower in Indians of low birth. When that strange race nears the dust and is condemned as untouchable, then nature remembers the physical perfection that she accomplished elsewhere, and throws out a god— not many, but one here and there, to prove to society how little its categories impress her. This man . . . stood out as divine, yet he was of the city, its garbage had nourished him, he would end on its rubbish heaps. Pulling the rope towards him, relaxing it rhythmically, sending swirls of air over others, receiving none himself, he seemed apart from human destinies, a male fate, a winnower of souls. . . . Something in his aloofness impressed the girl from middle-class England, and rebuked the narrowness of her sufferings. In virtue of what had she collected this roomful of people together?

The sexually frustrated Adela may indeed notice the punkah wallah's fine physique; his "aloofness" may even impress her, make her troubles seem insignificant, and cause her to question the virtue of the trial itself, but all that stuff in between? That, of course, is the narrator ventriloquizing his own interpretation. We know him well by now, and not only from his tonal register. We have come to expect him to dominate every scene, and we've gotten used to the characters not as props, but as lenses through which he frames his observations and speculations.

There's something so, I don't know, *imperious* about him.

I'm not here to reveal how an author comes up with a narrative strategy, mainly because every author works differently, but also because the process is not top-down. I'm sure a checklist exists online, but I'm afraid to look. I prefer to think that a story teaches its author how best to tell it, and that when a story simply won't get written, it's because the author's not listening.

I'm not naive enough to think that an author knows from the first word of a draft that the narrator will be so domineering, or that the inner lives of the privileged characters will be secondary to other, more sociopolitical concerns, or even that the book will have a three-part structure. Nor am I new-agey enough to think that an author can or even should dive into a story with no preconceived notion of how to tell it, ears cocked the better to receive its harmonic guidance. The best a writer can do is assess the effect each narrative decision has on a story, then decide if that's the effect she wants. A coherent and effective narrative strategy is the end result of a multitude of major and minor assessments and reassessments.

A story—a novel, in particular—is an imperfect thing. So, in the end, is a narrative strategy, no matter how airtight it appears, how neatly form and content complicate and complement each other. Too strict an adherence to a set of rules—even rules one sets for oneself—is dangerous in any art form, almost as dangerous as rejecting internal consistency altogether. As a brief coda to this chapter, in which I've stressed the importance of strict adherence to the narrative strategy, take this moment of potential discord in chapter 23 of *A Passage to India*. Here, Mrs. Moore is thinking about the move Aziz may or may not have made on Adela in the cave, and the echo (the "Boum") that she can't quite shake (italics mine):

> Nothing had happened, "and if it had," she found herself thinking with the cynicism of a withered priestess, "if it had, there are worse evils than love." The unspeakable attempt presented itself to her as love: in a cave, in a church—Boum, it amounts to the same. Visions are supposed to entail profundity, but—*Wait till you get one, dear reader!* The abyss also may be petty, the serpent of eternity made of maggots; her constant thought was: "Less attention should be paid

to my future daughter-in-law and more to me, there
is no sorrow like my sorrow . . ."

Here we have the first and only time our mile-high narrator directly addresses the reader. Is it a blip? A slip? A vestige of an earlier draft? An intentional disruption? In any of these cases, it violates what is an otherwise consistent set of narrative terms, breaking the fourth wall for no apparent reason. At worst, the move is arbitrary, an indulgence, a cheap way for the narrator to add drama and weight to the moment. But at best, it hands a key to the reader, one that may unlock that central mystery of the cave. At this point in the novel, the reader is not aware that the narrator, who's had access to everyone's minds and memories, who maps vast landscapes from his perch, will never reveal exactly what, if anything, "really happened" in the cave. Mrs. Moore's vision of love, elevated here by its coupling with the narrator's single instance of direct address, may be as close as we will get; it may be, in the end, the answer. Interpret the rest of Mrs. Moore's moment as you will—the petty abyss, the maggot-serpent of eternity, the self-pity of an old lady—because she won't speak again. The next day, she boards a ship for Britain and dies on the sea.

The Story(ies) of a Marriage

If there's a common denominator in the texts I've chosen for this book, it's that their narrative strategies continue to surprise and intrigue me, even and especially when they break their own rules, or when they signal a departure from the author's previous work. This is the case with Lorrie Moore's short story "Like Life," which, since its publication, in 1990, won't let me go. For a while, I couldn't figure out what it was, or how this story was different from the ones that came before it. Now I see that the answer has everything to do with narrative distance.

Lorrie Moore's early stories, especially those in her now-classic debut collection, *Self-Help*, have inspired numerous imitations. We may have *Self-Help* to blame—or credit, depending on your tastes—for the ongoing romance that fiction writers have with the second-person point of view, especially in stories of failed relationships or coming-of-age. Moore made second person look easy, and feel intimate, displaying a remarkable fluency with a point of view that smacks of self-consciousness and frequently comes off as a cheap and distancing device in the hands of a more self-indulgent narrator. Take this example from the oft-anthologized "How to Become a Writer":

> Decide that you like college life. In your dorm you meet many nice people. Some are smarter than you. And some, you notice, are dumber than you. You will continue, unfortunately, to view the world in exactly these terms for the rest of your life.

Moore's skill in *Self-Help* lies not only in articulating these sorts of everyday insights, but also in recognizing when they are better suited to second person than to the more traditional first or third. Not every story in the collection is told in the imperative mode, but passages like this likely explain why most readers remember *Self-Help* that way.

None of the stories in her follow-up collection, *Like Life*, are told in second person. Instead, Moore chooses an extremely close third in which the interior monologues and descriptions and metaphor-making are enmeshed in the main characters' voices and identities, and that makes frequent use of free indirect style. These narrators tend to be what we now consider classic Lorrie Moore: lost, lonely people, mostly women, sometimes with vague and troubling medical problems, spouting bon mots as they awkwardly bumble from relationship to relationship and through the seasons of life in familiar domestic or academic settings.

"Like Life," though, the title track of the collection, is notably more ambitious. It takes more risks with form and with content. As the final and longest story in the book, it can be seen as a hinge between what, for the sake of argument, I'll call Moore's "early story period" (*Self-Help* and the other stories in *Like Life*) and the collection that followed eight years later, *Birds of America*. In *Birds of America*, the stakes are significantly higher—in many cases, life and death—and the canvas more expansive, whereas the stories in the "early period" are primarily concerned with subtler shifts in romantic and family relationships. Moore imbues these relationships with emotional weight, invariably through heightened diction and metaphor. There is a richness to them even within the narrow worlds they inhabit. The stories are smart, frequently moving, and often hilarious slices of life, but, compared to her later work, they are smaller in scope and ambition: specific but not universal, individual but not societal.

As an example of this "rich narrowness," I think of Mary, the main character in "Two Boys," the first story in *Like Life*. Mary's big problem is her inability to choose between two sexually satisfying lovers: one a married and emotionally unavailable high-powered politician and the other an attentive but needy and poor hipster. (We should all have such problems, but I digress.) The tale is lyrically rendered, full of Moore's incomparable wit and stunning figurative language; its primary concern is not with larger cultural themes but with getting Mary right as a character, fine-tuning her perceptions and comic timing in the close third-person point of view in which it is told.

"Like Life" belongs more to the later era, in which Moore's tales become significantly darker and broader, and in which they take on more social or societal contexts and settings as much as individual experience. To accommodate this broader vision, Moore's narrators grow more distant. Or, as Moore's narrators grow more distant, their vision broadens.

Over the course of *Like Life*, Moore's narrators have trained readers to expect a collision with the main character in the first lines, and, as importantly, to stick exclusively with these characters throughout the rest of the stories, yoked to their every perception. See the immediate intimacy evident in the first lines from just three of these stories:

For the first time in her life, Mary was seeing two boys at once. ("Two Boys")

It was a fall, Jane knew, when little things were being taken away. ("Joy")

Harry lived near Times Square, above the sex pavilion that advertised 25 CENT GIRLS. ("Vissi d'Arte")

Until we reach "Like Life," the longest a narrator makes us wait for the inevitable collision with the main character is in "You're Ugly, Too" (italics mine):

You had to get out of them occasionally, those Illinois towns with the funny names: Paris, Oblong, Normal. Once, when the Dow-Jones dipped two hundred points, the Paris paper boasted a banner headline: NORMAL MAN MARRIES OBLONG WOMAN. They knew what was important. *They did!* But you had to get out once in a while, even if it was just across the border to Terre Haute, for a movie.

Outside of Paris, in the middle of a large field, was a scatter of brick buildings, a small liberal arts college with the improbable name of Hilldale-Versailles. Zoë Hendricks had been teaching American History there for three years.

Despite the chatty second-person narration that echoes the narration in *Self-Help,* and that short but significant line "They did!," the reader is not immediately aligned with a character until Zoë Hendricks appears in the second paragraph. Even then, though, we don't know for sure if she's the one who thinks, "You had to get out of [those towns] occasionally" or insists, "They did!," because we see her only from her department's collective perspective: "They felt she added some needed feminine touch to the corridors," and then from the dean's perspective:

> She was almost pretty, but her face showed the strain and ambition of always having been close but not quite. There was too much effort with the eyeliner, and her earrings . . . were a little frightening, jutting out from the side of her head like antennae.

To confuse matters even more, choice excerpts from Zoë's student evaluations are peppered throughout the beginning of the story, adding another dimension to our understanding of her character and the collective identities of the Midwestern coeds. All of these narrative signals—which point to a widening of the lens, an interest in something beyond the merely personal— suggest that the story will give us both a comprehensive view of Zoë and a fuller picture of the university and the ethos of Paris, Illinois.

And yet as the story unfolds, the narrator and the main character fuse in virtually the same way they have done in every other story in the collection, establishing a more intimate relationship. The reader delights in Zoë's skewering of the earnest, provincial Midwesterners she encounters in the classroom and on a series of disastrous dates. The dean's and students' perspectives never reappear; in fact, the reader assigns them retroactively to Zöe herself, self-assessing through their eyes. All the interior monologue and descriptions and perceptions belong to Zoë and Zoë alone, so that, by the end of the story, the only view of Zoë's world and of Zoë herself belongs to Zoë, unaltered by the series of events she's recounted, or by the suitor at the Halloween party she's just insulted. The story ends, as so many of Moore's stories do, in self-consciousness and ambiguity: "She smiled at him, and wondered how she looked."

As with the opening of *A Passage to India*, it's clear from the beginning that "Like Life" will take us into territory different in tone and subject matter from what has come before, in either of Moore's two collections to date. However, Moore's narrative strategy is not quite the same as Forster's. This story begins with an odd and intriguing eight-line epigraph credited to the long-forgotten 1951 elementary school textbook *A Child's History of Art.* "Suppose you had a choice of going to the circus / or painting a picture. Which would you choose?" the epigraph asks, then answers: "You'd choose the circus. / Everybody likes the circus."

It's worth noting here that an epigraph in itself creates distance. Like any outside text imposed on a work of fiction—including footnotes; historical documents;

photos; even, to an extent, maps and chronologies—it reveals, however subtly, the hand of the author constructing the reader's experience. Intentionally or not, the author interposes herself between the story and the reader, acting as a scrim or a lens, an organizing force.

After the epigraph in "Like Life" comes an opening that's arresting in its own right, but especially striking when compared to the tone, subject matter, and intimacy of the first movements of the stories that precede it in the collection. "All the movies that year were about people with plates in their heads," says the narrator, who then goes on to summarize the plots of a few of those movies, which immediately establishes an alternate and potentially fantastical setting. "Life seemed to have become like that," she continues. "It had burst out of itself, like a bug," the first of many plays on the title. The rest of the opening is worth excerpting in its entirety:

> In February a thaw gave the city the weepy ooze of a wound. There were many colds, people coughing in the subways. The sidewalks foamed to a cheese of spit, and the stoops, doorways, bus shelters were hedged with Rosies—that is what they were called— the jobless men, women, children with gourd lumps or fevers, imploring, hating eyes, and puffed lavender mouths, stark as paintings of mouths. The Rosies sold flowers: a prim tulip, an overflowing iris. Mostly no

one bought any. Mostly it was just other Rosies, trading bloom for bloom, until one of them, a woman or a child, died in the street, the others gathering around in a wail, in the tiny, dark morning hours, which weren't morning at all but night.

That year was the first that it became illegal—for those who lived in apartments or houses—not to have a television. The government claimed that important information, information necessary for survival, might need to be broadcast automatically, might need simply to burst on, which it could do. Civilization was at stake, it was said. "Already at the stake," said others, who had come to suspect that they were being spied on, controlled, that what they had thought when they were little—that the people on the television could also see you—now was true. You were supposed to leave it plugged in at all times, the plastic antenna raised in a V—for victory or peace, no one could say.

Mamie lost sleep. She began to distrust things, even her own words; too much had moved in.

It has taken a cryptic epigraph, five paragraphs, and a space break to get to the character of Mamie, who will become our main guide and whose perspective will shape the rest of the story. Until Mamie, the narration is oracular, the voice collective. The setting is a dystopian version of New York City in either the near or distant future, where people die in the street and television bursting on might be part of a government conspiracy to control your mind.

Are we really in Lorrie Moore Land here? Yes and no.

"Like Life" features everything the reader of *Self-Help* and the rest of the collection has come to expect from this author's work. As in "You're Ugly, Too," the main character and the narrator become virtually indistinguishable after she's introduced, fusing into one narrative voice in third person. It is Mamie who tells her own story, and, like many of the characters we've met in the two collections, she is an emotionally complicated and quippy, sarcastic, too-clever-by-half woman with a vague but threatening illness, trying to decide if the man in her life is the right one after all. She is the focus of every scene, dominating the dialogue and descriptions and internal monologues with surprising metaphors and other wry, witty wordplay. And finally, Mamie offers the usual abundance of aphoristic insights. "For love to last," she thinks, "you had to have illusions or have no illusions at all. But you had to stick to one or the other. It was the switching back and forth that endangered things."

In addition to all this, though, "Like Life" moves into distinctly different territory, and not just geographically. For a brief but crucial moment, Mamie's husband, Rudy, takes over the point of view; throughout the story, the dystopian outside world intrudes both literally and metaphorically into the action, also robbing Mamie of her perspective; the suspense of a murder mystery, of all things, hijacks the plot; and, perhaps most intriguingly, an epiphanic ending unifies the narrative and fulfills the contract the author sets forth in the first four paragraphs. I'd like to look more closely at these four departures to see how they demonstrate a shift in narrative range, and, ultimately, how that shift gives the story its transcendent power.

Mamie has lived with Rudy for ten years in the storefront of a converted beauty parlor, behind a padlocked door and boarded front windows. She longs for a real house—like the one with a bird feeder she glimpses on her way to the real estate agent's—and is wrestling with the prospect of leaving Rudy and moving into her own apartment. As a freelance children's historical illustrator, though, she can't afford to move. She's kept her desire to leave and her search a secret until, midway through the story, she tells him, "Rudy, I went to a realtor today."

> "Again?" Rudy sighed, ironic but hurt. Once love had seemed like magic. Now it seemed like tricks. You

had to learn the sleight-of-hand, the snarling dog, the Hail Marys and hoops of it! Through all the muck of themselves, the times they had unobligated each other, the anger, the permitted absences, the loneliness grown dangerous, she had always returned to him. He'd had faith in that—abracadabra! But eventually the deadliness set in again. Could you live in the dead excellence of a thing—the stupid mortar of a body, the stubborn husk love had crawled from? Yes, he thought.

Within a successful narrative strategy, point-of-view "slips" are rarely accidents; they often indicate a significant thematic moment, as we saw in *A Passage to India*. At the very least, they force the reader to question: Why here? Why now? In this case, Rudy's interior monologue is the first clear echo of the epigraph (the "hoops of it!") and points to what will become the story's central metaphor: their marriage, and maybe even marriage in general, as a dystopia. Mamie and Rudy's relationship *and* the outside world are the "stubborn husk" and "dead excellence" in which they are living—in which they are, in fact, barely surviving.

The distance established in the opening paragraphs and epigraph is what has granted the narrator "permission" to dip into another character's consciousness, however briefly. Such an intrusion, or slip, into

Rudy's thoughts would seem distractingly discordant—
arbitrary, at best—in a story in which the narrator fused
definitively and intimately with the character from the
opening lines. Another way of viewing this particular
strategic move is that Mamie's decision to bring the
moment to its crisis, to potentially end her marriage,
forces the narrative out of itself and aligns it with the
other principal player in the drama.

Immediately after Mamie's and Rudy's exchange, the
television flashes on automatically, "one of the government ads: pretty couples testifying to their undying de-
votion, undying bodies." These intrusions, which occur
periodically, add thematic emphasis as well as disrupt
any flow to the action and to Mamie's internal questioning. A wobbly disquietude follows as the couple struggles
to navigate the chasm that has opened in the wake of
Mamie's revelation. Eventually, they reach a moment of
tenderness; she puts her hand on his arm; he bends his
head to kiss it. The following passage ends the section:

> "Are you ever lonely?" Mamie asked him. Every
> moment of a morning seemed battled for, the past
> and future both seeking custody. She laid her cheek
> against his arm.
>
> "Mamie," he said softly, and that was all.
>
> In the last five years almost all of their friends
> had died.

The dystopian context, established by the oracular voice and coupled with grace notes such as this devastating line about the death surrounding the couple, gives what would otherwise be a conventional "bad marriage" story its unique urgency and metaphorical implications. The expanded distance, the widening of the lens, has allowed for this context, and thus its attending urgency. The distance keeps expanding and reestablishing itself throughout the story, incorporating not only the TV ads that keep popping up unbidden, like voices from the beyond, but also excerpts from the children's books Mamie is supposedly illustrating. The excerpts follow their own arc, unintegrated into Mamie and Rudy's story, about a Native American chief who dies from smallpox. The arc functions as another metaphorical lens through which to see this diseased world, this sick marriage.

As if this world weren't dangerous enough, a series of murders has occurred near the Gowanus Canal, and the specter of the murderer hangs over Mamie. One day, while she is walking home from the record store carrying a bag of cheap albums, still uncertain about her future with Rudy, Mamie watches a man fall from a bridge; a stranger tells her he's the man wanted for the Gowanus Canal murders. Mamie recognizes the falling man as Rudy. It's a climax unlike the others in the collection, occasioned by a twist in the plot rather than by a character's more subtle realization, revelation, or sense of loss. More interesting, though, than the surprise of this climax is how the narration changes to accommodate it. Up until this moment, Mamie's interiority has been its dominant mode, interrupted briefly by her actions of visiting her doctor and real estate agent, gazing upon her longed-for house, and processing her marriage with Rudy in dialogue. Now, suddenly, in Mamie's moment of crisis, when the focus of the story—her relationship with Rudy—comes to a head, the narration resists interiority. It switches to something like tunnel vision. Her one thought is *"No, not this."* In a long sequence, she drops her things, climbs onto the rail, tries not to look down. People speak to her. "Someone [is] touching her, clamping hands around her arms." She runs across the bridge, then twenty minutes to South Brooklyn, "through red lights and sirens," the narrator miles above her, until she gets to the bird-feeder house. When she arrives, breathless, she "[sinks] down on the concrete lip of its fence and [lets] out a cry, solitary and strangled, into her bag of songs." Eventually, she gets up and walks, "slow as an arthritic, clutching only her purse." She notices that the house with the bird feeder doesn't actually have a bird feeder, simply "a sign that said RESTAURANT, and there was a pigeon on it." She gives a dollar to a Rosie. When she gets home, another plot twist: Rudy is there. "'It's you,' Mamie [says], frozen by the open door."

It's at this moment, finally, that the spell breaks, and the narration fuses again with Mamie. Rudy asks, "Where have you been?" and she gives this wordless response:

> There was only this world, this looted, ventriloquized earth. If one were to look for a place to die, mightn't it be here?—like some old lesson of knowing your kind and returning. She was afraid, and the afraid, she knew finally, sought opportunities for bravery in love. She tucked the flower in her blouse. Life or death. Something or nothing. *You want something or nothing?*
>
> She stepped toward him with a heart she'd some-day tear the terror from.
>
> Here. But not now.

These are Mamie's thoughts, not those of the narrator that began the story; the filtering consciousness of "she knew finally" makes that clear. But the two voices share the same tonal register, unifying this epiphanic ending with the opening passage and with the intrusions of the outside world that have been occurring throughout, and that have contributed to the story's life-or-death urgency. All Mamie and Rudy have is each other; their only world is this wrecked one they are muddling through together. The flash-forward looks toward a certainty, rather than an ambiguity, about what's to come, and the narrator and character who have merged here now possess vaster knowledge about themselves and the nature of their relationship and the world around them than those in stories like "Two Boys" and "You're Ugly, Too."

The word *ventriloquized* is an echo of Mamie's earlier fear that objects have implanted themselves in her brain and might possibly be speaking for her. She fears that her whole body might come under someone else's control, be "approximated." In other words, she fears that she has lost, or will lose, the ability to tell her own story, to narrate her own life. This fear, and this echo of the fear in the final movement, calls attention to maybe the most significant and compelling of the distinguishing factors of "Like Life": it is a story, in effect, *about* narrative. It asks, subtly and explicitly, who speaks for whom, and why. It asks who determines and writes the story of a marriage, a life, a city, a country, in an age when and where one feels powerless, a subject of fate.

As in *A Passage to India,* what has allowed for this transcendence and broader vision, what has forced its revelations and richest metaphors, is its expanded narrative distance. Such expansion doesn't always make for a "better," more enjoyable or successful story, of course—if I had to pick between *A Passage to India* and *Howards End* to take to a deserted island, I'd choose the latter in a heartbeat—but, in the case of "Like Life," its more complicated and nuanced narrative strategy has distinguished it from the strict intimacy and "rich narrowness" of the other stories in the collection.

As we've seen, "Like Life" is a story that flirts with omniscient narration, then eventually settles into a more familiar and contemporary third-person limited. When I reread it, I'm seduced by the seemingly all-knowing voice all over again; I appreciate its broad strokes, its confident evocation of an age and setting. I'm almost disappointed when Mamie takes over and delivers the rest of the story, despite the thematic complexity the author achieves in that telling.

Much has been made of the twentieth- and early-twenty-first-century resistance to traditional omniscience in fiction. At the risk of being reductive, I think it's safe to say that the consensus on the matter is that, in Western literature, the omniscient narrator is too old-fashioned for a fractured world that distrusts authority, has abandoned God, and has little faith in any absolute truth put forth by an individual. Over the past century, as fiction itself has ceded much of its authority to film, television, and the Internet, the credibility of the writer—the novelist in particular—has grown increasingly suspect. The question goes: Who is she to speak for anyone or anything other than herself and her own experience?

And so, the consensus goes, relatively few writers dare to take on a godlike omniscience in their work. Instead, our charge has been to depict individual experience in its fullest and most vivid detail, keeping in the back of our minds that that experience is itself inherently limited. The literary merit we strive for lies in the depth, insight, freshness, and resonance of that limited portrayal. In reviews and book sales and blog chatter, the merit also seems to lie in whether readers can "relate" to the character, which really means whether they can recognize themselves in him or her.

These days, most of the novels said to have an omniscient point of view feature not an overarching godlike narrator, but multiple characters each taking turns in third person or first person. The space between those characters is sometimes, but rarely, occupied by an all-knowing voice or controlling consciousness like the one Forster employed in both *Howards End* and *A Passage to India;* instead, the privileged characters rub up against each other, and hand each other the mic, in chapters or sections demarcated by white space or helpful headings. The friction among the characters produces much of the meaning, which must be inferred or interpreted by the reader rather than provided by the omniscient narrator. In other words, the perspective is split among—but not shared by—the characters in the cast, each of whom delivers his or her own take on the events in due course. The effect is prismatic, in that the characters are distinct from each other but part of the same system. Whether they narrate in their own voices in first person or whether their voices are modulated in third person, the prismatic effect remains.

This strategy is the most effective way for the author to avoid claiming too much authority for herself; instead, she divvies it up among her characters. In that sense, the approach is quite different from what might be called a "nineteenth-century omniscience," in which the overarching voice or controlling consciousness, however wryly or subtly, instructs the reader how to see the characters and the worlds they inhabit. Embedded in those instructions is often a moral vision or judgment. It's no surprise, then, that most contemporary authors embrace the prismatic approach; it excuses us from the responsibility of exerting moral pressure, of formulating a broad social vision that might exclude entire swaths of readers.

Or does it? Ultimately, don't the author's vision and judgment lie in the final composition, in the unity of effect she has achieved by the story's end? The characters may have spoken for themselves along the way, each in turn, but only at the pleasure of the unseen author, and only for as long as she allowed them to hold the mic. To determine the moral imperative or broad vision of any text—and I believe every text has one, whether or not it is aware of its implications—the text must be considered as a whole, as the sum of its narrative parts. There may not be a chummy or imperious or oracular or cynical voice that serves as a stand-in for the author, but the text asserts its authority nonetheless.

In this way, every text—novel, story, memoir, film— has its own perspective, its own set of values and biases that are embodied by the author, modulated by the characters, and interpreted by the reader. This is true whether or not the author ever appears in the telling. After all, what is a vision but a "way of seeing" the world? And of what value is a story without a vision? Why bother to write if you don't have a view worthy of sharing? I think we judge the literary merit of a text not merely by how closely we relate to the characters' experiences—that's the relatively easy part of the author's job—but by how strongly the author's ultimate vision compels us, provokes us, challenges us, or makes new the everyday.

Late the other night, unable to sleep, I caught the pilot of the popular TV series *The Affair*, which, like Moore's "Like Life," is the story of a relationship on the rocks. A married man named Noah narrates the first half of the episode. He's looking back on the summer he met a young woman, Alison, with whom he had a torrid affair, and telling the story to an investigator, who interrupts the narrative to probe for details. The investigator's presence signals that something terrible has happened in the years since, but the viewer doesn't yet know what. In Noah's version of their first day together, he and Alison flirt with each other in the diner where she works as a waitress; he runs into her later at the beach, accepts her invitation to walk her home, and then spurns her bold invitation to join her in her family's outdoor shower. In the final scene, he watches from the end of the driveway as she's brutally raped over the hood of a car; when he starts to come closer to rescue her, the eye contact she makes with him urges him to retreat.

Then the screen goes dark, and the words "Part II: Alison" appear. The sun rises on the very same day, which we now see from Alison's point of view, up to and including the harrowing driveway scene. Alison is the one speaking to an investigator. Her version matches Noah's only in that the same key events occur: they meet in the diner; they run into each other on the beach; she invites him into the outdoor shower, they make eye contact as she's having sex in her driveway. The nature of the details, however, do not align. In Noah's version, Alison seduces him, first with a cigarette on the beach, then by stripping naked and stepping into the shower. In Alison's version, she's a forlorn mother grief-stricken at the loss of her only son, and she's tentative with Noah at best: it's he who offers to walk her home; it's he who tempts her with a cigarette; and while she does invite him to use her outdoor shower, the gesture, in her mind, is more neighborly than seductive. Finally, what Noah sees as a rape is Alison with her longtime partner, who, at her request, is doing his best to make her forget that today is their dead child's birthday.

This "he said/she said" narrative strategy calls attention, however blatantly, to the unreliability of memory, to the instinct for self-preservation, and to the inaccessibility of the truth. Both Noah and Alison believe their respective accounts of this fateful day, which paint themselves in the most sympathetic light possible. The "truth," or "what really happened" on that day—which could be either Noah's or Alison's version or, more likely, a hybrid of the two, complete with plenty of details both of them missed—remains forever inaccessible to them and to the viewer; there is no controlling authority to act as a narrator, to convince us and comfort us with the truth. The viewer is left destabilized, curious, anxious, and self-interrogating. The postmodern condition, perhaps.

Like "Like Life," *The Affair* is preoccupied with both the inner workings of a marriage and the nature and limits of narrative itself. As in so many stories with a prismatic narrative strategy—a few of which we'll look at in a later chapter in a more political context—the destabilizing absence of omniscient narrative authority is the point. Fiction writers keep making this point, whether we know it or not, in our resistance to the (re)assurance that omniscience offers, in our fear of saying something, of not just letting the text speak for itself. Taking their cue from the nineteenth century, and from a few too many English lit courses, contemporary readers are likely to conflate an omniscient narrator with the author herself. However, most of us don't want that responsibility.

No wonder that, when many writers are asked what book they love best, they go back to the nineteenth century, to novels no less complex and challenging and provocative than what's being published today, but more confident in their visions, and more comfortable with the burden of omniscience. I can think of a few of those novels and know-it-all narrators that made marriage their central subjects, that unpacked its politics, examined its role in society, charted its transgressions and joys and disappointments. And when I do—I can't help it—I miss them.

Try to See Things My Way

Every reader picks up a new book hoping to fall in love. We long for someone to take our open hand and lead us away, or astray, or under, or deeper into. During what we're aware will be a short time together, we trust this certain dashing someone to treat us right, and then, before it gets to be too much of a good thing, to leave us satisfied. This hand that takes ours invariably belongs to the narrator, who has seduced us page after page with with any number of winning traits: humor, shapely sentences, suspense, tension, insight, intellect, imagination, daring; the list goes, deliciously, on and on.

Sometimes, of course, we fall for the wrong person. He just screams danger. She's a bad seed. Whether we know it all along or figure it out partway through, we can't stop ourselves. We close our eyes, hold the hand tighter. Do with me what you will. I'm under your spell.

I'm not talking about the obviously unlikable characters, the villains, or even the antiheroes. Their repellent qualities, as well as their appeal, are easy to define and grasp. We can rationalize or intellectualize our attraction to them. Much has already been made of them in books and film and television—Humbert Humbert, Travis Bickle, Tony Soprano—why we love to hate them, which of our secret itches they scratch. We feel a guilty little thrill about cheering them on, and that transgressive pleasure keeps us rooting for them. If and when these bad guys (amazing, maybe, how often they are guys . . .) get their comeuppance, we take a different pleasure in their punishment, which validates or revises the world order. We've been absolved of some of our guilt for enjoying their misdeeds and also spared the punishment they've had to endure for committing them. It's easy to applaud justice when you don't have to do the time yourself. Instead we go back to our lives, in which we're mostly good to others and, if we're very lucky, our biggest problem is what to cook for dinner.

Some of these so-called unlikable characters are also narrators, and some of these narrators invite us to dislike them, even to reject them. Some *insist* that we do so, in fact, but their insistence and self-awareness are themselves forms of seduction; they're a dare, and who can resist a dare? Dostoyevsky may have been the first author of note to give us one of these characters, in *Notes from Underground:*

> I am a sick man . . . I am a wicked man. An unattractive man. I think my liver hurts. However, I don't know a fig about my sickness, and am not sure what it is that hurts me. I am not being treated and never have been, though I respect medicine and

doctors. What's more, I am also superstitious in the extreme; well, at least enough to respect medicine. (I'm sufficiently educated not to be superstitious, but I am.) No, sir, I refuse to be treated out of wickedness. Now, you will certainly not be so good as to understand this. Well, sir, but I understand it.

His "understanding" of his own situation is what compels us to keep reading, to find out what makes him tick. Also, we are drawn to anyone confident enough to show us his warts—or, in this case, his ailing liver—from the start; not only is it a refreshing change from most people we meet for the first time, but it suggests irresistible honesty and even integrity.

We meet a talky creature with a similar strategy 135 years later in Matthew Stadler's novel *Allan Stein.* Surely inspired by *Lolita,* Stadler's novel stars a predatory pedophilic narrator who warns the reader in the prologue that, in the account to follow, he "will lapse into coarseness, flippancy, lies, and pure pornography." Another dare, this one with the promise of sex. The narrator delivers and, time and again, periodically interrupts his own narrative to tell readers they should skip ahead if they don't want to read the particularly explicit part he's about to tell. I doubt anyone does. As with Dostoyevsky's narrator, we suspect that he's got some redemptive qualities somewhere, and we're willing to read for that potential surprise. Some of us even read for redemption, though we're afraid to admit it.

We admire Dostoyevsky's, Nabokov's, and Stadler's narrators for maneuvering us into a perspective we might not have agreed to have. We admire their self-creation and self-justifications, in which all three of them seem to revel. It may even be the reveling we admire most. We wish that, like Humbert Humbert in particular, we had such elaborate justifications for our own monstrous behavior, that which we do in secret, or that we fear we're capable of doing, or that for which we've been publicly excoriated. His is a lesson in self-delusion, and though there's no longer any hope for him, there may be hope for us.

But again, these unlikable narrators mostly fit the antihero mold, and their invitations to resist them are clear and successful ploys to come closer. What about narrators whose souls or agendas aren't particularly heroic? How do they still manage to entice and keep us? These unlikable sorts are much more difficult a breed to write than the antihero, though the two categories can blur. What makes them the best choice to tell the story?

Barbara Covett, the narrator of Zoë Heller's 2003 novel, *What Was She Thinking?*, is the teacher you avoid in the lunchroom. A bitter, acid-tongued, and judgmental unmarried woman in her sixties, she's taught history at St. George's, a British secondary school, for many decades. She befriends the new art teacher, Sheba Hart, who's young, earnest, beautiful, and living the upper-middle-class married life to which Barbara seems to aspire. Early in their friendship, Barbara learns that Sheba is having a rather torrid and reckless affair with a fifteen-year-old student, Stephen Connolly. Jealous and disapproving, Barbara urges Sheba to cease the affair, but Barbara is so desperate for Sheba's friendship that she uses their shared secret as a way to keep her close and solidify their bond. Ultimately, though, Barbara hastens Sheba's undoing, which includes the destruction of her marriage, criminal charges, and her shameful seclusion in Barbara's house—under Barbara's strict care—as she awaits trial.

Speaking in first-person present tense and directly addressing the reader throughout, Barbara makes the case for herself early on that she is the "best qualified" person to write the story of Sheba's "downfall." She alone, she tells the reader, can provide the finely detailed account of what happened between Sheba and the Connolly boy, both because Sheba "doesn't seem to tire of [telling her] the story" and because Barbara herself has been keeping an exhaustive diary of everything that's happened. "I am not so foolhardy as to claim for myself an infallible or complete version of the story," she says, and yet that's just what she does, time and again, casting herself as the sole reliable authority and using both Sheba's words and her own diary as evidence. She's even marked key dates with gold stars; the more stars, the more crucial the events on that date.

But all these declarations of Barbara's legitimacy as narrator are, at best, unnecessary. She is under no obligation to justify her telling of this or any tale, to prove its reliability in advance or even to document its provenance. The success or failure of the tale will be in how she tells it, not in whether she has successfully earned the right. And so we can almost hear the machinery click on when she tells us, in the foreword, "Once [Sheba's] got her drink, she relaxes a bit. . . . You wouldn't believe how many times she is willing to go back over the same small event, examining its details for clues and symbols." The same goes for the device of the diary, which makes for clunky chapter transitions: "The last Friday in March marked something of a turning point in my relations with Sheba. I have given the date one gold star." Both the justifications and the diary are an index of Barbara's obsessiveness with all things Sheba, but that obsessiveness is so well established by Barbara's actions that everything else is overkill.

What makes all the machinery unnecessary? The fictional dream itself. In this dream, into which every reader of fiction enters, we instinctively suspend our disbelief that the elements of the story—of any story—

can be remembered with perfect accuracy, let alone coherently and vividly arranged. Such is the power of the narrator in fiction (and memoir, for that matter): rarely is the reader forced—or even prompted—to question how the narrator came by her tale or the details that give it specificity, resonance, and meaning. The dream allows us to instinctively trust her. The dream is its own justification. The narrator gains authority by the simple act of convincing us, scene after scene, of what's being said, done, and felt by the characters. By calling attention to her legitimacy, then, Barbara undermines it. She disrupts the dream. Such self-sabotage may serve a thematic purpose, but it's one that's been obvious from the start.

As narrative strategies go, though, Barbara's is remarkably effective despite its inelegance. Ultimately, what makes it so convincing is not how she got her information, or how accurate it is, but the voice in which she delivers it. This is a voice committed to unrelenting fierceness—one marked by withering sarcasm, self-pity, anger, and gallows humor—and it demands that we believe it. So deep and consistent is Barbara's commitment to her vision of the world in which she is both victim and hero that we can't help but respect it, even and especially if we recognize much of it as a delusion. And because she directs some of her harshest invective at herself, her particular brand of monomania doesn't turn us off or shut us out. It's a familiar but effective trick of self-presentation: forestall blame by being your own worst critic. As transparent as it may be, it's a tried-and-true way that an "unlikable" narrator establishes credibility and engenders sympathy, and I'm frequently surprised by how little the transparency matters. A little self-hatred goes a long way.

It's no wonder, then, that on the day Barbara finally betrays Sheba, in what is arguably the turning point of the novel, she is at her most self-effacing. She has been asked to lunch on a Saturday by a fellow teacher, Brian Bangs. Though she considers him "a fool," she also recognizes, "who was I to pick and choose?" Then, briefly, she allows herself to dream of a different life for herself, one in which she "would cease to be the shut-in biddy waiting around for an invitation from [her] one, married friend"; she would finally become "a person who had easy relations with the world, a person who spent [her] weekends having dates, who carried photographs in [her] wallet, documenting scenes from . . . jolly parties and rowdy barbeques and delightful christenings." She sees, briefly, in the absurd Bangs, a respite from "the drip, drip of long-haul, no-end-in-sight solitude" of which "Sheba and her like have no clue":

> They don't know what it is to be so chronically untouched that the accidental brush of a bus conductor's hand on your shoulder sends a jolt of longing

straight to your groin. I have sat on park benches and trains and school room chairs, feeling the great store of unused, objectless love sitting in my belly like a stone until I was sure I would cry out and fall, flailing to the ground.

But any hope of respite disappears for Barbara when Bangs confesses that he has a crush not on her, but on Sheba. Humiliated, she acts out by telling Bangs of Sheba's affair, an act she knows will eventually lead to her friend's destruction. This is how she rationalizes her behavior:

> Chance is everything, isn't it? I so nearly didn't go to Bangs's flat, and then, when I did, I so nearly left before I said anything damaging. It seems to me that an enormous amount of vice—and virtue for that matter—is a matter of circumstance. . . . Evil will out, my mother used to say, but I rather think she was wrong about that. Evil can stay in, minding its own business for eternity, if the right situation doesn't arise.

However harshly we may judge either woman's behavior, we can't help but admire Barbara's ability to assess the situation—every situation, in fact—in a way that simultaneously elevates, excuses, and dismisses her role in it. Barbara's complex psychology is the heart of the novel, the engine that drives every scene; we keep reading as much to see what she'll think next as to see what will happen next. Moments before Bangs confesses his crush, she shares with the reader "the real source of [her] dismay" in life, which is her "irrelevance," her sense that she neither belongs nor matters. She realizes that people like Bangs are always confiding in her not because she is important, but because she is "so outside the loop, so remote from the doings of the great world, as to be defused of any possible threat. The number of secrets I receive is in inverse proportion to the number of secrets anyone expects me to have of my own." The betrayal in itself is an interesting plot twist, but more interesting is the context Barbara gives it in her narration; it's her context that gives it weight. Without Barbara's perspective, the betrayal is just the next episode in the soap opera.

When Barbara leaves Bangs on that fateful day, it's to collect her beloved cat, Portia, from the vet. Portia has been sick for a while, and has taken a sharp turn for the worse. The vet wants to put her down, but Barbara begs him to give them one last night together. She fries Portia sausages in butter. She curls herself around her on the eiderdown. Then, for the first and only time in the novel, she cries:

> Although, because mourning . . . is never the focused, unadulterated business we pretend it to be, my tears

were only partly for Portia. Once the engine of grief
was revved up, it began ranging, as grief tends to,
about the crowded territory of my other discontents
and regrets. I cried from guilt and remorse that
I had not been a better, kinder pet owner. . . . I cried
because I had dealt what seemed to me an almost
certainly fatal blow to my friendship with Sheba. I
cried because I had been desperate enough to consider a liaison with a ludicrous man who collected
baseball jackets and even he had rejected me. . . .
I cried, finally, at the indignity of my crying, the sheer
stupidity of being a spinster blubbing in her bedroom
on a Saturday night. . . .

Shortly after that, my commitment to my own
misery began to wane, and I stopped being able to
focus. In the end, I turned on the television and, for
half an hour before I fell asleep, I watched the evening news, utterly dry-eyed.

Barbara constructs her narrative so that we feel sympathy for her, and we do; a dying cat is a quick and arguably cheap route to such sympathy. But it's a queasy
sympathy, at best, and it's the queasiness that saves
this scene from pure sentimentality, and that continually saves Barbara as narrator from the reader's rejection. The salacious tale of Sheba's affair with the boy
is, by the end, a red herring; her soap opera is far less
interesting than how Barbara constructs it, interprets it,

and inserts herself into it. Barbara's version of events, stuffed with dark insights into everything from the nature of her own character to politics, grief, history, longing, and sex, *is* the story; you encounter her twisted wisdom on every page. As in *Lolita*, the plot, such as it is, plays second fiddle to that fireworks display of psychology. Barbara Covett is not as linguistically inventive as Humbert Humbert, and she's as sexually repressed as he is sexually ferocious, but her narration—more than the diary she supposedly keeps—is, like his, a riveting document of obsession.

The old adage "He who represents himself has a fool for a client" may apply just as well to fiction as to the law. From the court of point of view, a character who narrates in first person exposes herself to a greater degree than she would in third person. The relative distance of third person gives her cover; and, of course, as we have seen, even within third person the narrator can modulate that distance.

With the intimacy of first person comes a vulnerability for which there is little or no cover, and with that vulnerability comes both a more exciting opportunity to win the reader's engagement and a higher risk of rejection. Vulnerability is what makes the first-person point of view well suited to the so-called unlikable narrator; ironically, it also makes her more likely to be considered unlikable in the first place. There's an anxiety to even the most confident first-person narrator, talking naked before an empty room, that readers simultaneously identify with and resist. When that narrator is recounting the cruel and unpleasant things she did, our moral judgment (which kicks in almost immediately) validates that anxiety and creates a comfortable distance. We are no longer participants in the drama, but voyeurs.

A creature less odious than Barbara Covett or Humbert Humbert—someone more winning, say, more traditionally likable—has less to prove; her dance of blame and rationalization is less intricate. In other words, it's not quite as much fun to watch. It was certainly foolish of them to expose themselves the way they did—we wouldn't recommend it if, god help us, they were our friends—but what a guilty pleasure it is, what a dream, to be taken into their confidence, to be seduced into seeing things their way.

Readers require a great deal of first-person narrators, especially those who dare to misbehave. We demand more from their voices: more humor, more style, more insight. We are less forgiving of tangents and sidetracks; we want them to be in control. If they're going to spend all this time barking into our ear, they better do it with some grace and ambition, and they better have something to say. Most importantly, we better not get the sense that their story would have been more effectively told using a different strategy, that it required a wider lens or a broader perspective or multiple voices to achieve the resonance it attempted. When we read a story or a novel in first person, we still demand completeness—or, at least, fullness—from what is essentially a fragment. You don't get to the end of *Lolita* and think *something's missing.*

If there's a privileged main character in Faulkner's *Light in August,* we're not confident we know who it is by the end of the first five chapters, which is roughly a quarter of the novel. In this long exposition, the voice is relatively restrained in its narration of the thoughts and actions of various characters. Using a strategy similar to Forster's in *A Passage to India,* the third-person narrator of *Light in August* sits above the action and uses language and diction far beyond the characters' capacity, fuses with them from time to time, then pulls back. Unlike Forster's, the narrator appears neutral, telling the story without judgment or bias or a clear agenda other than to capture the totality of the experience.

Then, at the start of chapter 6, the narrator changes the game:

Memory believes before knowing remembers.
Believes longer than recollects, longer than knowing

even wonders. Knows remembers believes a corridor
in a big long garbled cold echoing building of dark
red brick sootbleakened by more chimneys than its
own, set in a grassless cinderstrewnpacked com-
pound surrounded by smoking factory purlieus and
enclosed by a ten foot steel-and-wire fence like a
penitentiary or a zoo, where in random erratic surges,
with sparrowlike childtrebling, orphans in identical
and uniform blue denim in and out of remembering
but in knowing constant as the bleak walls, the bleak
windows where in rain soot from the yearly adjacent-
ing chimneys streaked like black tears.

I vividly remember the first time I read this passage.
It ignited me. I brought my face closer to the page to
absorb it. I was a college freshman, a bit excitable and
just beginning to understand the limitless possibilities
of language. (I'm still just beginning.) I wrote a paper
on it and got a D. It was a theory course, where fawn-
ing over lyricism and beauty and supercool invented
words like *cinderstrewnpacked* wasn't encouraged. Like
many creative writers, I bristled at theory. All of that
"death of the author" stuff, not to mention the clinical
reduction of my favorite novels and poems to "texts,"
struck fear in my buoyant little heart.

Anyway, when I reread this passage in *Light in August*
now, I still admire Faulkner's singular voice, but I also

notice the important role the passage plays in the novel's narrative strategy. In addition to its thematic resonances—memory, faith, knowledge—it functions as a line of demarcation between the book's first movement, which takes place mostly in present action, and the very long flashback that will take up the next eight chapters. It marks a clear tonal shift in its use of abstractions like "memory" and "knowing" as subjects; in its absence of character; in its excessive use of unpunctuated series of adjectives and verbs; and in its cluster of invented words like *sootbleakened, childtrebling,* and the like in one paragraph. The relatively conventional narrator of the first five sections seems to be transforming—or fading—before our eyes. The move signals a significant transition.

The narrator who takes over brings us the heart and soul of *Light in August:* the story of Joe Christmas. He is one of those orphans in blue denim; those "black tears" may be his as well. By virtue of the airtime he gets in the long middle section, the consistent narrative fusion that occurs throughout it, and the complexity of his psychology, he becomes, unquestionably, the privileged character on whom the novel centers.

He also does some pretty awful things.

The novel asks us to understand why, or at least how, Joe became the kind of man who brutalized women from a young age, potentially killed his foster father, and murdered his lover, Joanna Burden. To achieve this understanding, the narrator essentially becomes Joe for those middle chapters. He immerses himself fully in his world, seeing it through his eyes from his childhood through his young adulthood. He continues to tell the story in third person and in his own elevated diction, which helps maintain an overall tonal unity with the rest of the novel, but otherwise we hear Joe's voice in dialogue and the occasional italicized interior monologue. With the decrease in distance between Joe and the narrator comes an increase in intimacy and vulnerability. While *A Passage to India* and "Like Life" expanded their narrative distance in order to accommodate the authors' and narrators' broader visions, *Light in August* contracts, zooming in on Joe Christmas in order to make a stronger case for his essential humanity.

The centerpiece of the narrator's case is the formative trauma—a version of a "primal scene"—that the innocent and heretofore undamaged Joe endures in the orphanage. A child, "small even for five years, sober and quiet as a shadow," Joe sneaks into the dietitian's room to eat from the tube of toothpaste she keeps on her washstand. He's been doing this undetected for a year, one little "pink worm" of the stuff at a time, but today the dietitian enters the room with her lover and he's forced to hide under the curtain. He takes the tube of toothpaste with him and, as the lovers go about their furtive and frenzied business, he over-indulges in eating too much of it. And then, "in the rife, pinkwomansmelling obscurity behind the curtain he squatted, pinkfoamed, listening to his insides, waiting with astonished fatalism for what was about to happen to him."

What happens is that he vomits, and the dietitian discovers him. She thinks him a spy, and, afraid she'll lose her job if he snitches, flies into a rage:

> "You little rat!" the thin, furious voice hissed. "You
> little rat! Spying on me! You little nigger bastard!"

What happens is that, for the first time, an adult has made him aware of his racial difference; and there he sits in a pool of his own vomit, awash with shame and fear, surrounded by the smell and touch of women's undergarments.

Over the next few days, the dietitian's rage turns to frantic paranoia. She gives Joe a dollar, which confuses him utterly. He can't comprehend her system of punishment. He has never had any intention of telling on her; he doesn't even realize there's anything to tell. "He was waiting to get whipped and then be released." Eventually, unable to endure what she considers Joe's psychological torture, the dietitian conspires with the janitor and the matron to get him sent away from the orphanage. In the matron's office, the first words Joe hears from his adoptive father are "Christmas. A heathenish name. Sacrilege. I will change that." The stranger goes on to say, "He will eat my bread and he will observe my religion. . . . Why should he not bear my name?"

This extended primal scene, which spans twenty-five pages and the rest of chapter 6, and which takes place immediately after the "Memory believes before knowing remembers" paragraph, is the authoritative account of the formation of Joe's identity. As such, it becomes the lens through which the reader will view Joe for the rest of the novel. It's important to note that, in his account, the narrator not only includes Joe's experience of coming into his precarious identity—a black boy who can sometimes pass as white, a kid named Christmas now suddenly called McEachern, a godless orphan conscripted into a strict religion—but also details how the cruel figures around him have determined his fate. There's the janitor, a religious fanatic, who considers him "evil" and kidnaps him; there's the "flabby faced" matron, with her "weak, kind, frustrated eyes," who, once the dietitian reveals Joe's mixed race, immediately places him elsewhere; there's the dietitian herself, who tells anyone who will listen that the other children have been calling Joe "nigger" for years, which may or may not be true; and, of course, there's Joe's punishing adoptive father. Versions of these four figures will continually reappear throughout the novel in various forms, repeating history, recasting the orphanage trauma, always in that same intersection of racial identity, sex, and religion. Joe struggles to feel anything but anxiety and fear in his own skin; he is rootless and restless, incapable of trust; he commits violent acts, mostly against women. The reader recoils at Joe's brutality, but in part because the narrator invests the childhood trauma from which that brutality derives with such vivid and detailed specificity, we do not reject him. We have been made to understand how he has come to feel simultaneously "like an eagle: hard, sufficient, potent, remorseless, strong" and that "like the eagle, his own flesh as well as all space was still a cage."

Early childhood trauma is not the secret ingredient in fiction that makes the unlikable narrator sympathetic or even readable. You don't just add it to a story like a roux to a gravy, expecting it to thicken and add depth. In fact, too often in fiction, trauma—any "formative" incident, really—has a too-facile one-to-one correlation with character identity and behavior. The author asks us to base our entire interpretation of a character on that incident, which frequently involves some form of physical or sexual abuse, psychological scarring, grief, or, at the very least, a really mean mother. I've been guilty of this on more occasions than I care to admit. What interests me about *Light in August* is not how Faulkner transcends the one-to-one correlation (which he does, thrillingly, in ways far beyond the scope of this book) but how the effective telling of Joe Christmas's story requires that subtle but distinct shift in perspective.

Every narrator occupies a kind of bully pulpit, a clear position of authority granted by the simple fact of her existence. Barbara Covett and the narrator of *Light in August* use their bully pulpits to make their respective cases: Barbara to legitimize herself and rationalize her behavior, Faulkner's narrator to explore extensively the origins of Joe Christmas's identity. They drive the narrative in their writerly way, using the tools of craft, manipulating distance, showing and telling, to achieve their desired effects. Writers too often underestimate just how bullying the narrator's pulpit actually is, how much influence she wields over readers, and how unforgiving and disappointed readers can be when we sense that the narrator's grip on her material isn't as tight as we'd hoped.

For most of our early lives, the people who tell us stories are the people we trust most; often, they're the people we love most. And these people we respect, trust, and love tell us some crazy stuff: *leave this tooth under your pillow, and in the middle of the night a fairy will bring you money; Goldie the goldfish swam from the toilet to the ocean to play with her friends; we're almost there; I'll always be here for you; someday you'll look back on this and laugh.*

I believe that the initial trust we have in the story-teller makes a deeper imprint than any eventual disappointment. And so, as readers and listeners, we instinctively trust the narrator; it's in our nature. At the very least, we go into a story assuming we can trust her until she gives us a clear reason not to.

To take it a step further, I believe we *want* to trust the narrator, that it taps into a place in us we may have lost, that we open a book already seeking a storyteller in control.

≡

"I shall say things to you I've said to no one before. I found no reason for doing so until now. I have decided to do so lest your imagination run away with you—since you have studied poetry."

The speaker here is Mustafa Sa'eed, one of two first-person narrators in Tayeb Salih's extraordinary and enduring novel *Season of Migration to the North,* first published in Arabic in 1966. The other narrator is the unnamed student of poetry—he has a doctorate, in fact, from a British university—who has returned after many years to his village along the Nile in Sudan. He narrates the majority of the book, but it is Sa'eed's story, told in first person but in three separate sections, that haunts and obsesses him and that forms the more dramatic account.

Sa'eed is immediately a figure of fascination and mystery for the narrator, whom I will hereafter call "the scholar," both for clarity and to highlight one of Mustafa's first taunts. "We have no need of poetry here," he tells the scholar in their first substantial conversation. "It would have been better if you'd studied agriculture, engineering or medicine." Sa'eed knows whereof he speaks. He, too, has studied in Great Britain and returned to his native country. It's one of the many anxieties that pulse throughout this postcolonial novel: Of what use is the colonizer's education in this newly liberated nation? What positive and lasting effect, if any, can/will the scholar have on the people and homeland he left behind?

The scholar eventually takes a civil service job in the ministry of education, but is largely ineffectual and indecisive in his role. He has opinions, but little courage to defend or act on them. His own education has not prepared him for the kind of decisions that must be made both culturally and politically. In the meantime, Sa'eed dies, presumably in a flood. The scholar receives a letter from him that appears to be both suicide note and will. Sa'eed has entrusted him not only with his story, but also with the care of his wife and sons; tragically, though, he is incapable of successfully filling that role as well.

The scholar's story is one of passivity and paralysis— "All my life I had not chosen, had not decided," he says, in the final scene—while Sa'eed's is defined by action. Like Joe Christmas, Mustafa Sa'eed terrorizes women; in Britain, he drives three of them to suicide; he cartoonishly exaggerates his "otherness" to seduce them and validate his professors' and mentors' impressions and biases; he murders his wife, Jean Morris, by stabbing her in the chest; and yet, ultimately, it's the scholar who earns our scorn.

We dislike him not just because he's passive, but because he's not as good a storyteller.

It's not as if a passive character can't make a compelling narrator. Clarissa Dalloway doesn't do much with her day but throw a party, but when Virginia Woolf's freefloating narrator merges with her long enough to bring us the world the way she uniquely senses and remembers and longs for it, the particular way in which she *loves* it, what is more transfixing? All Clarissa has to do is think—something Salih's scholar is perfectly capable of doing, especially given his doctorate in poetry—and out comes a rush of feeling lush and lyrical enough to keep any reader breathlessly on the page:

> Such fools we are, she thought, crossing Victoria Street. For Heaven only knows why one loves it so, how one sees it so, making it up, building it round one, tumbling it, creating it every moment afresh; but the veriest frumps, the most dejected of miseries sitting on doorsteps (drink their downfall) do the same; can't be dealt with, she felt positive, by Acts of Parliament for that very reason: they love life. In people's eyes, in the swing, tramp and trudge; in the bellow and the uproar; the carriages, motor cars, omnibuses, vans, sandwich men shuffling and swinging; brass bands; barrel organs; in the triumph and the jingle and the strange high singing of some aeroplane overhead was what she loved; life; London; this moment of June.

While Mustafa Sa'eed's narration isn't nearly as lyrical as Woolf's speaker's, its charged style is marked by the use of poetic images, rhythms, and patterns; he uses repetition, in particular, to quite powerful and dramatic effect. His high style distinguishes his narrative from the scholar's. Sa'eed is also in much more conscious control of language itself in his timing and metaphor-making and use of sensory descriptions, basking in the use of the colonizer's tongue and the colonizer's literature to advance his desires, which are a passionate mix of sexual and intellectual:

> "My mind was like a keen knife. But the language is not my language; I had learnt to be eloquent in it through perseverance. And the train carried me to Victoria Station and to the world of Jean Morris."

A page later, in reference to Ann Hammond, one of the women he drove to suicide:

> "The room was heavy with the smell of burning sandalwood and incense, and in the bathroom were pungent Eastern perfumes, lotions, unguents, powders, and pills. My bedroom was like an operating theatre in a hospital. There is a still pool in the depths of every woman that I knew how to stir. One day they found her dead. She had gassed herself. They also found a small piece of paper with my name on it. It contained nothing but the words: 'Mr Sa'eed, may God damn you.' My mind was like a sharp knife. The train carried me to Victoria Station and to the world of Jean Morris."

Two pages later, during his trial:

"It occurred to me that I should stand up and say to them: 'This is untrue, a fabrication. It was I who killed them. I am the desert of thirst. I am no Othello. I am a lie. Why don't you sentence me to be hanged and so kill the lie?' But Professor Foster-Keen turned the trial into a conflict between two worlds, a struggle of which I was one of the victims. The train carried me to Victoria Station and to the world of Jean Morris."

Sa'eed is telling this story directly *to* the scholar, who has (fairly easily) coaxed it out of him. Despite his claim that he has never told his story to anyone else, Sa'eed wants his story to be heard, and he considers the scholar a worthy listener and kindred spirit, if only by virtue of their similar Western education and status as fellow migrants. It's possible that he believes that the scholar is the only person who will understand it in all its implications.

The author sets off the two stories graphically by giving Sa'eed's tale quotation marks; he also separates the first installment of Sa'eed's story from the scholar's by giving it a chapter of its own. But these efforts at differentiation, while effective, are hardly necessary: when Sa'eed speaks, the prose comes alive; when the scholar speaks, the prose is relatively workaday, his voice deliberative and flat. For contrast, here is the scholar's narration after he fails to prevent the tragedy that leaves Sa'eed's widow dead:

> The world has turned suddenly upside down. Love?
> Love does not do this. This is hatred. I feel hatred
> and seek revenge; my adversary is within and I needs
> must confront him. Even so, there is still in my mind
> a modicum of sense that is aware of the irony of the
> situation.

This flatness effectively characterizes the scholar as a man without distinction. He has no name and his voice no signature. From the moment he returned to Sudan, he has been seduced and, in effect, diminished by Sa'eed's voice, by the power of his actions and his ability to describe those actions. The irony is not lost that much of the power of Sa'eed's tale comes from his lyricism, derived apparently from the poetry he deems useless. The author's narrative strategy requires that the "lesser" storyteller, the scholar, narrate most of the book because, otherwise, Sa'eed's intensity would threaten to overwhelm it. Without the contrast, the difference in the two men's political and sexual efficacy would not be as apparent.

The intense climax of Sa'eed's story is placed at the end of the novel, far out of chronological sequence but very much in the scholar's psychological sequence. Having reached a point of reckoning, the scholar finally visits Sa'eed's house, specifically the locked room that holds the memorabilia of Sa'eed's time abroad, all of his letters and photos and papers. When the scholar comes upon an image of Jean Morris—whose importance has been emphasized by Sa'eed's haunting refrain—the last act of the drama is finally unleashed.

Once again, Sa'eed takes over the narration, this time in the middle of the page, not set apart in a separate chapter. He calls himself, among other things, "the invader who had come from the South," and Jean Morris "the icy battlefield from which [he] would not make a safe return." One dark February evening, he leaves the station for home, seething with the history of degradation that he and Morris have inflicted on each other in a kind of mutually assured annihilation, and finds her "stretched out naked on the bed, her white thighs open." The reader has been well prepared for what is about to happen; South and North have had this date with each other from the beginning:

> "Here are my ships, my darling, sailing towards the shores of destruction. I leant over and kissed her. I put the blade-edge between her breasts and she twined her legs round my back. Slowly I pressed down. Slowly. She opened her eyes. What ecstasy there was in those eyes! . . . I pressed down the dagger

with my chest until it had all disappeared between her breasts. I could feel the hot blood gushing from her chest. . . .

"We were a torch of flame, the edges of the bed tongues of Hell-fire. The smell of smoke was in my nostrils as she said to me 'I love you, my darling,' and as I said to her 'I love you, my darling,' and the universe, with its past, present and future, was gathered together into a single point before and after which nothing existed."

Often, an unlikable character "fails" not because he lacks winning qualities, but because he's not a good narrator. Unlikability, then, is the narrative strategy that misfires, if not from the start, then somewhere along the way. The truly unlikable narrator is in the book you put down, the one who doesn't ignite or engage you. That book is sitting on your nightstand right now, unfinished, abandoned. Effective narration is about control, and using the bully pulpit to maximum effect, and manipulating distance and intimacy, but mostly it's about language, about the shape of the line, the sound of the voice. More than plot, it is language we fall hardest for, that seduces us most potently, that makes the best case, that maintains its staying power over the course of a work of fiction and long after the story ends. Dynamism in language, a lyrical seduction, is the common denominator among all of the so-called unlikable narrators I admire—Heller's, Faulkner's, Salih's—and, of course, Dostoyevsky's and Stadler's and Nabokov's, Nabokov's maybe most of all. Where would Humbert Humbert be without the poetry of his prose?

In the final chapter of *Season of Migration to the North*, after Sa'eed's bloody tale is told, the scholar walks naked into the Nile. As a way of cleansing himself of rage, he resolves to swim for the northern shore, but soon the river's "destructive forces" pull him down. He feels himself succumbing to these forces, and for a moment we think he will, but then he suddenly experiences "a violent desire for a cigarette." His mind clears. "Now I am making a decision," he thinks. "I choose life." He has "a few people [he wants] to stay with" and "duties to discharge." He will live "by force and cunning." Sa'eed's narrative has inspired him, you might say, if not to murder or violence, then to action. To embrace life. Perhaps to embrace poetry. Flailing in the water, "like a comic actor shouting on a stage," he screams his last words: "Help! Help!"

The Position of Power

In her TED talk "The Danger of the Single Story," Chimamanda Ngozi Adichie reminds us that "the problem with stereotypes is not that they are untrue, but that they are incomplete. They make one story become the only story." Her focus is on literature specifically and media in general, and she argues that when a particular group—a nation, a culture—is shown as one thing, "as only one thing, over and over again," then "that is what they become."

As a reader and writer who might describe myself (or be described by others) as gay, Italian, or any number of other identifiers, I take Adichie's talk as a call to action. As a reader, she tells me: be promiscuous in your choice of stories that are set in other countries, or that represent cultures and experiences different from your own; seek a wide range within each country or group; and don't allow yourself to be convinced of any group's essential ethos.

This doesn't work, though, without a kind of negative capability, a peacemaking with the indisputable fact that, no matter how many books and stories and other media we consume, we will never know *anyone's* full story. Walt Whitman, my first love, said it best:

When I read the book, the biography famous,
And is this then (said I) what the author calls a
    man's life?
And so will some one when I am dead and gone
    write my life?
(As if any man really knew aught of my life,
Why even I myself I often think know little or
    nothing of my real life,
Only a few hints, a few diffused faint clews and
    indirections
I seek for my own use to trace out here.)

I have barely a grasp on my own "real life," my family's, my country's. How can I expect to feel comfort in my knowledge of a people across the ocean, or the group in the church behind my house? So it's not comfort that I expect, but the grace of empathy, that endlessly renewable resource found in every honest story.

This is what Adichie's speech says to me as a writer: you have more of an obligation than you thought you did. If your gay character reinforces a stereotype, or your fictional Italian American family acts like every other Italian American family, you are guilty of perpetuating a single story. You are part of the problem.

As if I didn't feel anxious enough. As if freshness and authenticity weren't already my concerns and those of every writer I know. Still, we can't feel it too keenly or too often, that push to tell the honest story with as much complexity and insight and invention as we can, to shine a light into the dusty corners of human experience, to resist the most accessible images, to make the specific universal and the universal specific; in short, to honor the power that perspective grants us.

If it's a given that stories exert power, that they effect change in the world in immeasurable ways, then who tells the story occupies the most powerful position of all. It is the author's position, of course, but, as her proxy, her narrators' as well. Who tells a story claims responsibility for it. In devising and drafting a narrative strategy, an author makes all sorts of craft decisions that influence how the work will be read and enjoyed, but these technical decisions become deeply social and political when she gives over the narrative reins to someone on the margins, or who might otherwise be despised, or who has been invisible. Every college student assigned *Wide Sargasso Sea* after *Jane Eyre* immediately grasps the political implications of giving the "madwoman in the attic" the power to tell her story her way.

The relationship between the author's unique background and status to that of her narrator(s)—and characters in general—is, to put it mildly, highly charged. The question of how far outside her own experience an author is "allowed" to write has more to do with politics than with craft; as such, it is outside the scope of this book. But since I did introduce politics, I'll let Grace Paley speak for my take on the issue. When Paley was asked about negative reactions to stories she wrote "in a black voice," she responded:

> But what's a writer for? The whole point is to put yourself into other lives, other heads—writers have always done that. If you screw up, so someone will tell you, that's all. . . . Men have so often written about women without knowing the reality of their lives, and worse, without being interested in that daily reality.

In this book, and in this section in particular, I'm less interested in whether a writer can or should write from a perspective different from her own than in how the narrative strategy changes when writers from groups outside the so-called mainstream claim perspective for themselves. I am focusing on three writers—Grace Paley, Tim O'Brien, and Tony Kushner—who may not be widely considered "out of the mainstream," but whose work, like Adichie's, both subtly and directly takes on this question of power.

I met Grace Paley in May 2005, two years before she died. A longtime fan of her short stories, I'd invited her to Boston to deliver the keynote speech at a literary conference I was organizing. She arrived by bus, wearing sneakers and a small backpack, double-strapped, and waited patiently in an armchair in the lobby of the hotel while I pitched a fit at the desk because her room wasn't ready. "This is one of our greatest living writers!" I barked. "And she's just *sitting there!*" I fretted and paced for over two hours, growing increasingly hysterical, asking Grace again and again if she needed anything. But she just shook her head and smiled. In the meantime, writing students and fellow authors recognized her—at eighty-two, with her familiar corona of white hair and soulful, observant eyes, she was hard to miss—and literally knelt beside her. Often she laid a hand on theirs as they spoke. She asked about their writing, and the Walk for Hunger taking place in Boston the next day, and the war in Iraq. Instead of going straight up when her room was ready, she stayed in her chair talking to the group that had formed on the carpet in front of her. Later, on our way to the fancy dinner we threw in her honor, she did finally make a request, the only one of her visit. She'd forgotten a comb. We picked one out together, and in the window of a CVS a block from the fancy restaurant, she teased up her locks.

This little anecdote captures some of Paley's humility and generosity and whimsy, but not her fierceness. All are evident in *The Collected Stories,* which features primarily female narrators in conversation with each other, their families, their lovers, and the reader. The speakers are almost uniformly like Grace. They are women who speak their minds, concerned less with the urgency of getting from here to there—the plot, so to speak—than with responding to what surrounds them in the moment: the demands of friends and children and men and art, personal desires and disappointments, social injustices of all kinds. The conversation is constant, continually interrupted, rarely resolved. Some stories come across more like fragments, one side of a dialogue overheard through a Bronx window, or an excerpted monologue delivered into a mirror or a bullhorn.

Reading Paley's *Collected Stories* straight through for the first time, rather than dipping into the stories here and there, I expected the fragments of the mosaic to form a whole picture; maybe I even expected a sneakily buried through-line of a plot; but instead I felt even more intensely that I was being bombarded by bursts of strong, bright voices from a world I could overhear but not fully enter. This was true even though the same speakers show up from time to time, and more than a few of the ones who don't reappear sound a lot like them and/or Paley herself. There is certainly coherence—the same author writing in similar voices on many of the same themes, with great clarity and insight—but not completeness.

Paley was not only conscious of this strategy; she owned it; you might even say she invented it. One of her most-quoted passages is from "A Conversation with My Father," in which a man expresses frustration with his daughter's refusal or inability to write a traditional narrative, a "simple" Chekhovian story about people and "what happened to them next" (a more "male" story, one presumes). His daughter, the speaker, thinks, rather cheekily, that she would indeed like to tell that kind of story, except that it requires a plot, "the absolute line between two points which [she's] always despised. Not for literary reasons, but because it takes all hope away. Everyone, real or invented, deserves the open destiny of life."

What's despicable about the absolute line between two points is its danger of becoming a single story. For Paley, there was no "defining" experience of women or Jews or New York or activists or the 1960s, or of one female Russian Jewish activist-writer in New York in 1965. There were stops and starts, inconsistencies, loyalties forged and broken, discordant voices. People made themselves up as they went along. In the meantime, there was daily life to endure. All of this became the stuff of her fiction. Paley's reverence for the "open destiny of life" is her reverence for these nuances of everyday experience, which do not fit into neat lines. To do right by her mostly female characters, to honor their individuality and give their domestic experience the legitimacy and gravity it was not receiving elsewhere, required a strategy that privileged speaker over story, anecdote over epiphany.

Paley's stories often begin in midconversation, midsituation, or midthought, rarely with much context or long descriptions of the weather or a catchy "hook" designed for suspense. If the reader is hooked, it's by the quiet force of the narrators' voices and the situations in which they find themselves:

> The old are modest, said Philip. They tend not to outlive one another. ("Dreamer in a Dead Language")

> My husband gave me a broom one Christmas. This wasn't right. No one can tell me it was meant kindly. ("An Interest in Life")

> No doubt that is Eddie Teitelbaum on the topmost step of 1434, a dark-jawed, bossy youth in need of repair. ("In Time Which Made a Monkey of Us All")

> I saw my ex-husband in the street. I was sitting on the steps of the new library. ("Wants")

From these casual but crafted openings flow narratives without clear direction. The absence of quotation marks contributes to this sense of flow among thought, voice, and action; it also gives the impression that there is no controlling authority imposing order on the various anecdotes and conversations. The stories seem willed into being by some unknown force, or, at the very least, "happened upon" by the reader. This is a false impression, of course. The flow is not a blur. Even in her most elliptical stories, Paley's narrators speak with perfect lucidity, and it's always clear who's talking and to whom.

The body of the story "Wants," for example, is the conversation between the speaker and her ex-husband after she sees him from the library steps. The exchange is shot through with both the tenderness and the bitter recriminations of a couple with a lot of water under the bridge. But to appreciate fully the logic of the couple's case for and against each other and their marriage, the reader must decode the subtext between them; it's our job, in partnership with an active but not controlling narrator, to fill in the gaps and the transitions. This demand on the reader is also part of what saves Paley's stories from being classified as mere anecdotes; despite her supposedly "light" domestic concerns and her wry humor, there is nothing breezy or quick in the experience of reading her.

Here is the ending of "Wants," which Paley read as part of her remarks that afternoon in Boston in 2005:

I wanted to have been married forever to one person, my ex-husband or my present one. Either has enough character for a whole life, which as it turns out is really not such a long time. You couldn't exhaust either man's qualities or get under the rock of his reasons in one short life.

Just this morning I looked out the window to watch the street for a while and saw that the little sycamores the city had dreamily planted a couple of years before the kids were born had come that day to the prime of their lives.

Well! I decided to bring those two books back to the library. Which proves that when a person or an event comes along to jolt or appraise me I *can* take some appropriate action, although I am better known for my hospitable remarks.

As in the work of her descendants Lydia Davis and Amy Hempel, among many others, every word by every speaker in this and each of Paley's stories has fought for its place on the page. The attention this precision of language requires from the reader subtly implies that the speaker's words matter, and, more importantly, that the experiences her words illuminate are not only valid, but vital. In this way, one can view Paley's strategy of conversations and fragments, which eschews traditional plot and the standard payoff of an epiphany, as subversive not only in its documentation of the often invisible experience of women's lives at the time, but in its redistribution of narrative power into the voices of speakers who use it "merely" to recount the challenges of their daily lives.

A guy named Tim narrates *The Things They Carried*, "a work of fiction" by a guy named Tim O'Brien. Taught in literature, history, and creative writing classes alike, *The Things They Carried* is widely considered a classic testament of Vietnam, an authoritative guide to the horror of war, and a meditation on "story" itself. War and story are the two central subjects of the twenty-two chapters of varying length that constitute the collection. Like Paley's stories, O'Brien's feature an abundance of anecdotes and fragments, but, unlike Paley's, they are filtered through one perspective—Tim's, in first person—and many of them follow quite closely that "absolute line between two points" that Paley resisted. Rather than give his characters "the open destiny of life," O'Brien fixes them in event after event, some with resolution and even morals, all while questioning the insufficiency of both.

The title story, placed first, introduces the main characters, Tim's fellow soldiers, by cataloging what they literally and figuratively strap to their backs as they trudge through the jungles of Vietnam. It's the only story told in omniscient third person, but retroactively the reader understands not only that Tim is the narrator, but that he likely had to invent some of the details in order for the story to resonate. Similar to the first movements of *A Passage to India* and "Like Life," the title story draws the boundaries of an expansive territory for the narrator—the minds and histories of the guys in his platoon, the blurry intersection of truth and fiction—while establishing his authority and his voice. The difference is that throughout the collection Tim makes his own narration (and narration in general) a character in the drama, analyzing its nature in metafictional passages directed at the reader, passionately trying to convince us that, even and especially if Tim does make up some stuff along the way, he is still speaking the truth.

In "How to Tell a True War Story," the centerpiece of O'Brien's metafictional strategy, Tim intersperses his definitions of "war story" with multiple iterations of the death of Curt Lemon, its effect on his friend Rat Kiley, and other stories that spin off from the telling of that particular tragedy. The meaning derived from the interplay between the definitions and the stories themselves is possible only with a narrator who has demonstrated intimate knowledge of his material. Tim never tells us *who* can tell a true war story like this—who has permission—only *how.* The proof of authenticity, and

maybe even the permission, are in the unflinching specificity of the details: the exact word—*cooze*—that Rat
Kiley calls Curt Lemon's sister when she doesn't respond
to his heartfelt letter; the song—"Lemon Tree"—that
Dave Jensen sings as he and Tim throw down Curt's
parts from the tree he is "sucked" into after the gre-
nade explosion; the baby buffalo Rat shoots, one body
part at a time, until all that's left of it are its still-moving
eyes, "which were enormous, the pupils shiny black
and dumb." These details are specific enough to create
their own truth. "True war stories do not generalize,"
Tim tells us. "They do not indulge in abstraction or
analysis." Every good storyteller knows this, but it's especially important when the details are matters of life
and death.

We trust Tim's narration not only because he's
taken the name of the author and has even mentioned,
at least twice in the collection, that he's "forty-three
years old, and a writer now"; that claim of credibility
via autobiography gets a narrator only so far. We trust
Tim because he convinces us with details, from the
weight—down to the ounce—of each and every item
the men carry to the "smell of moss" at the trail junc-
tion and the "tiny white blossoms" in the tree beneath
which Curt and Rat are goofing off with grenades. The
details are not limited to objects or to the senses, but
extend to dialogue and to the emotional toll the war

takes on the soldiers. "Send guys to war, they come home talking dirty," Tim tells us. "Listen to Rat: 'Jesus Christ, man, I write this beautiful fuckin' letter, I slave over it, and what happens? The dumb cooze never writes back.'" Rat cries as he shoots the buffalo, tries to talk about it, can't, then goes off by himself. Tim observes: "We had witnessed something essential, something brand-new and profound, a piece of the world so startling there was not yet a name for it."

"How to Tell a True War Story" stands alone and is often anthologized, but it makes its deepest impact when it is read amid the unrelenting stream of stories that come before and after it in the collection. "How to Tell a True War Story" is a primer on how to read these other stories and evaluate their teller. Nowhere is this more evident than in the comprehensive cataloging of the title story, which we learn to read, in part, as the narrator's attempt to impose order on senselessness.

As in Paley's work, it's the fact that there are so *many* stories and details—such a multitude of voices, anecdotes, moments of beauty and love and horror and grief—that seems crucial to O'Brien's project. Stories erupt within other stories, revise and sometimes negate themselves, explain their own origins, jump forward and back in time, confess and retract, implicate and vindicate; most importantly, though, they just keep coming. "You can tell a true war story if you just keep on telling it," Tim tells us, moments after he's admitted that he's invented everything he's just told us about the death of his fellow soldier:

> No Lemon, no Rat Kiley. No trail junction. No baby buffalo. No vines or moss or white blossoms. Beginning to end . . . it's all made up. Every goddamn detail—the mountains and the river and especially that poor dumb baby buffalo. None of it happened. *None* of it. And even if it did happen, it didn't happen in the mountains, it happened in this little village on the Batangan Peninsula, and it was raining like crazy, and one night a guy named Stink Harris woke up screaming with a leech on his tongue.

Tim's narration, while always controlled, is almost manic in its desire to tell not just one true war story, but as many as he can; at the very least, he wants to thoroughly document the effects of war before, during, and after combat, which often involves making up a lot of stuff. In fact, the invention of detail may be *required* to achieve the truth he seeks; it may even be required to achieve truth in our own lives. It is O'Brien's choice to interweave this sort of commentary on narrative itself—to make story and truth subjects in question— that makes *The Things They Carried* an implicit critique of any reliance on a single story. He has instilled in the reader a productive distrust of any one war story, no matter how vivid and enduring, including his.

The characters in Tony Kushner's *Angels in America*—mostly gay men—are soldiers in their own battles, fighting their own vicious demons in New York, Salt Lake City, and "Elsewhere." Part I was first performed in 1991, Part II a year later, and the film adaptation that combined both parts, directed by Mike Nichols, appeared in 2003. Because Kushner himself wrote the screenplay, making judicious revisions to what frequently stretched to a seven-and-a-half-hour stage production, and because the film is now easily accessible and has been watched by millions, it stands as the definitive version of what is frequently called the most significant play of the twentieth century.

Though there is sometimes a guiding narrator or narrators who break the fourth wall—like the stage manager in *Our Town*, a quite different distinctly American tale—most plays are told in the objective point of view. Interiority is externalized, delivered as a monologue or an aside or spoken directly to the audience. This doesn't mean that "no one" tells the story, or even that "everyone" tells the story; the playwright in his notes, the director, the set designer, among many others, including the actors, have collaborated to determine the narrative strategy that forms the audience's viewing experience. For Kushner, this strategy had something to do with the viewer's self-conscious astonishment: "It's OK if the wires show," he writes in "A Few Notes from the Playwright About Staging," published in the print version, but "the moments of magic . . . ought to be fully imagined and realized, as wonderful *theatrical illusions*" and "at the same time be thoroughly thrilling, fantastical, amazing." With its big budget and high production values, the HBO film certainly aims for amazement, but not self-consciousness. Telling the story his way, Nichols hides the wires. The result is a version much less raw than the original, slicker, starring some of the greatest mainstream actors of the time (Al Pacino, Meryl Streep, Emma Thompson) rather than the no-name actors at the Eureka Theatre, in San Francisco, in 1991. The shift from relative rawness to mainstream big-money luster mirrors the explosion of "gay stories" in literature, television, and film between the early 1990s, and 2003. Suddenly, it seemed, everyone was telling them, and they weren't all so dire.

Angels in America centers on four gay male characters: Prior, Louis, Joe, and Roy. Their story lines intersect and are interdependent—the plot relies on their influencing, seducing, betraying, and/or loving each other—but each man has a story of his own, and each tells his story in his own words. There is no definitive main character, though Prior gets a bit more airtime, is visited by the all-important angel in the climax of Part I, and speaks the last words of the epilogue, delivered directly to the reader/viewer:

> We won't die secret deaths anymore. The world only
> spins forward. We will be citizens. The time has come.
> 　Bye now.
> 　You are fabulous creatures, each and every one.
> 　And I bless you: *More Life.*
> 　The Great Work Begins.

Similarly to Paley's and O'Brien's work, *Angels in America* invests in multiplicity, in a cross section of voices and perspectives and angles. Louis, Prior's boyfriend, leaves him when he can no longer handle the horror of Prior's worsening illness; Roy, the closeted antigay attorney, fights disbarment and his own HIV diagnosis while trying to lure Joe into the political fold; Joe denies his homosexual urges and his increasingly detached wife, before falling in love with Louis. Kushner chooses not to tell just one of these characters' stories; he resists the creation of a definitive, or even a "specific but universal" Portrait of AIDS as a Young Gay Man, in favor of a significantly broader, more ambitious project.

As part of its narrative strategy, *Angels* does impose some limits on that broadness. Actors play multiple parts, including characters of the opposite gender, which is a way of letting the wires show while advancing the theme of interconnectedness. Each main player is a facet of a distinctly American experience: Joe is a devout Mormon, that homegrown religion; Roy is Roy Cohn, the notoriously and virulently antigay chief counsel to U.S. senator Joseph McCarthy; Prior descends from *Mayflower* stock. Together with Louis, a Jewish leftist, and Belize, a former drag queen turned nurse, these men form something of a composite—though far from complete—picture of the gay man in Ronald Reagan's America.

In assembling these characters, Kushner reveals his unique vision of a place and time and group; he also wants his characters to say something about the American experiment, politics, history, and religion. Such a project requires not only a bigger canvas—more of a diorama, actually—but also, in this case, multiple storytellers, each with his own take on what makes a (gay) man in America. Though the play, ultimately, has a hopeful ending—we are all "fabulous creatures," and our "Great Work" begins now!—its more cynical takes and realities, articulated with force and conviction by the narrators, stand alongside the optimism, creating friction. In fact, the play's success relies on the uneasy coexistence of those narrators and their unique truths. Prior's optimism in the final lines does not negate the voices of the men who have come before him. The voices of these two especially:

BELIZE: Well I hate America, Louis. I hate this country. It's just big ideas, and stories, and people dying, and people like you.

The white cracker who wrote the National Anthem knew what he was doing. He set the word "free" to a note so high nobody can reach it. That was deliberate. Nothing on earth sounds less like freedom to me.

You come with me to room 1013 over at the hospital, I'll show you America. Terminal, crazy and mean.

I *live* in America, Louis, that's hard enough, I don't have to love it. You do that. Everybody's got to love something.

ROY (to his doctor): Your problem, Henry, is that you are hung up on word, on labels, that you believe they mean what they seem to mean. AIDS. Homosexual. Gay. Lesbian. You think these are names that tell you who someone sleeps with, but they don't tell you that. . . . Like all labels they tell you one thing and one thing only: where does an individual so identified fit in the food chain, in the pecking order? Not ideology, or sexual taste, but something much simpler: clout. . . . This is reality. I have sex with men. But unlike nearly every other man of whom this is true, I bring the guy I'm screwing to the White House and President Reagan smiles at us and shakes his hand. Because *what* I am is defined entirely by *who* I am.

Roy Cohn is not a homesexual. Roy Cohn is a hetero-
sexual man, Henry, who fucks around with guys.

Okay, well, so what? Lots of stories have multiple
narrators, a large cast of principal characters, and political themes, some of which conflict. You can probably name five before you reach the end of this sentence.
But I think there's a difference that's common to Paley's
Collected Stories, O'Brien's *The Things They Carried*,
and *Angels in America*. In all three, the narrators par-
ticipate in the dominant system but belong to groups
that are invisible, dispossessed, misrepresented, mis-
understood, feared, and/or vilified; more importantly,
they are compelled, for whatever reason, to be comprehensive—or, at least, "representative"—in the telling of
multiple stories from multiple angles within their respective groups. There's an anxiety of obligation to this
multiplicity, an inherent and likely subconscious fear
of perpetuating a single story. There may also be an
implicit discomfort with the responsibility and power
of perspective itself, of owning and defining an experience or identity that is still in the process of gaining
visibility, civil rights, compassion, and recognition.

My first clear image of a gay man was a skeletal Rock
Hudson on television in the summer of 1985, flashbulbs
going off around him, while newscasters speculated on

the cause of his rapid decline. I was thirteen. I don't remember if I knew what AIDS was until that moment, or if I even understood that "gay" was an identity, but, from then on, one became synonymous with the other, and together they equaled that diseased, emaciated figure once so handsome and beloved.

Soon after, I was at a friend's birthday party at the bowling alley down the street from my house. As I waited my turn, chatting with my friends, the world suddenly detached. I sensed I was floating away from the scene in front of me, as if I'd become a ghost, or maybe my friends were the ghosts and I'd crossed into their alternate universe. I broke into a sweat; my heart pounded; still I went on talking—no one noticed I felt any different—waiting for the world to right itself. It did right itself, after a few minutes, but later that night, alone in my room, it happened again, that sudden detachment, and then again the next day, and on multiple occasions every single day afterward. I didn't tell a soul.

My lifeline was the blue pages of the phone book, which listed free numbers and codes I could use to listen to prerecorded messages about various illnesses: "schizophrenia," "multiple personality disorder," "homosexuality." These were the same words I looked up in the card catalog at the local library, but that was riskier. Instead, I took out film histories, searched the glossy middle pages for photos of Rock Hudson, and gazed morbidly at the man he once was. I filled my journals with desperate pleas to God to heal my afflictions: the freaky disassociation, the aching desire I felt for the boys in my class and the handsome man in the photographs. In the meantime, I kept waiting to go crazy enough on the inside for someone to notice. I kept waiting to rot from the outside. I didn't know which would happen first, only that both were inevitable.

I had based my identity on a single story. A tragic story, no less, made more powerful in its vividness and melodrama and indelible detail. Other less tragic, maybe even happy, narratives of the lives of gay men certainly existed in the mid to late '80s and early '90s— *Angels in America,* of course, debuted in 1993 in New York, two hours north of my home—but either they were inaccessible or I willfully resisted them.

We take a great risk when we change our narrative, when we tell a different story about ourselves to ourselves. No wonder we do it so seldom, if at all. Tell yourself a story for long enough, and it comes to define you. You settle into it. There's a comfort in the single story, one as potent as the danger.

Shifting Perspective

There is no shortage of excellent writing advice. Like most of us, I'm better at quoting it than at taking it. And surely you've noticed I haven't offered much of it. My goal has been to ask questions of the narrator, mostly how and why, through the lens of craft. In doing so, I've tried to reconstruct the process writers go through when the first glimmer of a story appears in our heads, looking for its shape and voice, auditioning, sometimes begging to be told, sometimes playing hard to get.

"The Philly Story"—remember that? I don't blame you; it's been a while—is one of those glimmers for me. I've been writing *The Art of Perspective* to figure out how best to tell it, and how best to evaluate the many others like it that have appeared in the meantime, and that will keep appearing. With the completion of each chapter, I've seen these glimmers grow larger and closer and come into focus, shiny with possibility and promise, only to fade away again. Writers live in a fog periodically lit by such glimmers.

Drafting "The Philly Story," I auditioned chummy unnamed omniscient narrators like Forster's in *Howards End,* narrators who have aligned themselves with Christopher or Michael or Charlene and explored the emotional connections among them, and who bear a striking resemblance to the author. But that felt too pretentious, and the individual histories too diffuse, too arbitrarily connected. I tried a more expansive approach, titled "The City of Brotherly Love," which took a more historical view, rooting the events in the ideas of independence and freedom. Somewhere in that version, Ben Franklin appeared in a dream. It didn't work. I worried over each character's potential unlikability: in some versions, one of the men is an ogre; in others, Charlene is a thief, and not one with a heart of gold. Those got melodramatic. I felt anxious about misrepresentation, which brought me back to a more personal take, a first-person account from Christopher's point of view that drowned itself in self-indulgence.

So I tried, I really did, here and there. But not hard enough. I was doing it the easy way, the cowardly way. By that I mean I was afraid to commit a single word to the page. All the drafts I wrote have been in my head. They had a perfectly fine time there, too, gathering meaning, morphing into a poem or an essay for a time, hitting dead ends, changing course and color, retreating. They kept me company. They were becoming, in all senses of the word.

I'm not proud of this. It's immature and more than a little embarrassing. I've always longed to be more like Tennessee Williams, who rarely met an idea he didn't try to work into a play, poem, story, or letter, or Sylvia Plath, who, according to Ted Hughes, took an "artisan-like" approach to her poems: "if she couldn't get a table out of the material, she was quite happy to get a chair, or even a toy. The end product for her was not so much a successful poem, as something that had temporarily exhausted her ingenuity." At my peril, I've ignored one of those excellent pieces of writing advice a friend once quoted me: Don't hoard your stories. Get them out, she said, on the page, and put everything you've got into each one, all your best lines and metaphors and ideas. Then move on to the next story, which will come only if you've given everything to the one before it. The assembly line approach, she called it, which works for both the novel and the short story. Apparently, the brain defies natural law: the more you scoop from it, the more there is to scoop.

But I admit it, I'm a hoarder. I'm not afraid just to finish a story—to force upon it one immutable destiny— I'm afraid to *start* one, to produce its ugly early versions, its malformed incarnations. I understand the necessity of the process, but I don't have to like it.

For all of this anxiety, I blame perspective, specifically its refusal to keep still. In the year since Michael and I met Charlene on Thirteeth Street, the way I see that encounter has changed. My perspective on it will likely change again and again over the years, and we will both change along with it. When will I know if I have the "right" perspective to make the best possible story from that raw material? And, if I do find the "right" perspective, will it lead me reliably to an effective narrative strategy?

When you're a writer, people often advise you not to make your subject matter something you're "in the middle of"—a divorce, an illness, grief over the loss of a loved one—because you can't see it clearly; "you don't have the perspective on it yet," they say, often with a hand on your shoulder. But how do you know when you're no longer in the middle of something, even something that's not a tragedy? Does perspective just appear one day on your doorstep, drop its bags, and stay for a spell? If so, for how long?

It's also conventional wisdom that writing *leads* you to perspective, that processing the grief you're mired in will lead you from the muck to a safer, more comfortable place from which you can look back in relative peace. This is the definition of perspective as mountaintop oasis, art as catharsis. As much as I'd like to, I don't quite buy this, either. Time and distance certainly help us along, working together to provide insight into our past selves. For example, as a kid I didn't link my panic attacks to Rock Hudson or to my potential sexual identity; never once did I connect the two; they were just the twin crosses I was given to bear, one on each shoulder.

It's only in hindsight that I see the obvious link, that I make the connection between two things that I was too young or enmeshed in to connect at the time. We all know that it's nearly impossible to create this sort of narrative at all without such perspective, and that the process of shaping and telling ourselves and others the story is itself a kind of solace. So is creating a fictionalized version of that kid, one wildly different from myself, but using the linkage to inform his character and give him a different destiny. Any solace we feel comes from the act of ordering and organizing experience that had once been amorphous, uncontrollable, ineffable, and incomprehensible. All of that's a given. All of that is, well, life.

Making sense of our lives by turning our experiences into narrative—especially by dramatizing and offering insight on the terrible things that have happened to us and the people we love—gives us something to do, an outlet and a distraction, and a sense of power; but these are fleeting at best, and the power is crushingly false. Our loss remains as immense as when we began. The only difference is that now we've gotten a new toy out of it. I've got a whole set of those toys in my file cabinet, and you probably do, too.

Many years ago, after reading a dear friend's beautiful and moving essay on the death of her father, I naïvely asked her if writing it "helped her put his death in perspective." This writer is the gentlest soul I know, but the face she turned to me was filled with rage. I see her face whenever someone recommends a writing workshop to a person who's suffered a tragedy. It is like recommending travel, an endeavor undoubtedly valuable and worthwhile, but one that can never erase the loss you have come to it to escape. "I pack my trunk, embrace my friends, embark on the sea," Emerson wrote, "and at last wake up in Naples, and there beside me is the stern fact, the sad self, unrelenting, identical, that I fled from."

We can think of perspective as a mountaintop oasis, but only if we remember that the mountain is always moving, that the view from the ledge is ever changing. The writer's goal is not to derive comfort from the trek across the sea and up the mountain, but to document that view with honesty and integrity once she gets there. In other words, to use the tools of craft to tell the story with as much urgency and insight and style and depth as she can. In that telling is, of course, where the art of perspective lies.

One of the primary reasons I'm afraid to commit a story to the page, let alone finish it, is that the years have taught me how subtly and profoundly the view will shift. I fear that, at some point in the future, possibly even overnight, I'll find I lacked sufficient insight. That my style has become more sophisticated since then, that my capacity for depth is now greater. Or that I got it just plain wrong. So, of course, the story is much safer in my head, glimmering and untold.

The big problem is that, of all the crimes a writer can commit, playing it safe is among the most unforgivable.

This is true: a year, almost to the day, after Michael and I met Charlene, two guys, twenty-seven and twenty-eight, walked out of their downtown Philly apartment near Thirteenth Street to grab a slice of pizza. On the way, three people their age, two guys and a girl out with friends, attacked them, unprovoked. According to the police report, the fight started after one of the guys in the group asked, "Is this your fucking boyfriend?" and ended with the attackers bashing in their faces and leaving them in a pool of blood on the sidewalk. The guys survived, but one was beaten so badly the cops assumed he'd been shot; he had to have his jaw wired shut for six weeks. The story shocked the city and the otherwise peaceful neighborhood. At the time of this writing, the attackers are awaiting trial.

I wish I could tell you my first reaction wasn't *that could have been us.* I wish I could say I didn't then, almost immediately, consider how this horrible and very real tragedy both shrank and expanded the fictional possibilities of "The Philly Story." I wish I could say I wasn't grateful that I hadn't already written and submitted my version somewhere. This additional source material, as awful and heartbreaking as it is, gives me the opportunity to invent a better story from my own, one with deeper resonances. I know from Forster and from Lorrie Moore that if—when—I end up finally committing the story to the page, it will require a wider lens. I have a clearer sense of who might tell it, and how. I still don't know if I've arrived at the "right" point, if this is the view I want to preserve—but my gut tells me I should give it a try.

It also reminds me of this: who tells the story—the author and his proxy, the narrator or narrators—is often vulturous. He feeds on misery and complications as much as on connection and revelation. She's always looking for the point of entry and the point of no return, the moment of transformation and of (self-)destruction. Trouble. Suffering. Redemption, too, on occasion. Love, when it's in danger. His honesty can be both ruthless and generous at once. You can't trust him one bit, especially if you believe him.

Acknowledgments

The greatest joy of working on this project has been my ongoing conversation with Charles Baxter. If there is anything useful in these pages, surely it came from him.

I am also grateful to Fiona McCrae for her sharp editorial eye, and to Janet Silver, Liz Braun, Nathalie Anderson, Rachel Pastan, Stacey D'Erasmo, Jesse Aron Green, Maud Casey, C. Dale Young, Stephen McCauley, Michael Borum, and the entire team at Graywolf.

A few chapters began as classes at the Bread Loaf Writers' Conference, the MFA Program for Writers at Warren Wilson, and GrubStreet, where many wise students and colleagues informed the discussion.

Thank you to the MacDowell Colony for the fellowship that allowed me to complete the first draft.

Works Referenced

Adichie, Chimamanda Ngozi. "The Danger of a Single Story."

Brontë, Charlotte. *Jane Eyre.*

Dostoyevsky, Fyodor. *Notes from Underground.*

Eliot, T. S. *The Waste Land.*

Faulkner, William. *As I Lay Dying.*

Faulkner, William. *Light in August.*

Forster, E. M. *Howards End.*

Forster, E. M. *A Passage to India.*

Gardner, John. *The Art of Fiction.*

Gornick, Vivian. *The Situation and the Story.*

Heller, Zoë. *What Was She Thinking?*

Johnson, Denis. "Emergency."

Kushner, Tony. *Angels in America.*

Lardner, Ring. "Haircut."

McEwan, Ian. *Atonement.*

Moore, Lorrie. *Birds of America.*

Moore, Lorrie. *Like Life.*

Moore, Lorrie. *Self-Help.*

Nabokov, Vladimir. *Lolita.*

O'Brien, Tim. *The Things They Carried.*

Paley, Grace. *The Collected Stories.*

Rhys, Jean. *Wide Sargasso Sea.*

Salih, Tayeb. *Season of Migration to the North.*

Stadler, Matthew. *Allan Stein.*

Walker, Alice. *The Color Purple.*

Whitman, Walt. *Leaves of Grass.*

Wilder, Thornton. *Our Town.*

Woolf, Virginia. *Mrs. Dalloway.*

Woolf, Virginia. *Orlando.*

Woolf, Virginia. *To the Lighthouse.*

CHRISTOPHER CASTELLANI is the author of three critically acclaimed novels: *All This Talk of Love, The Saint of Lost Things,* and *A Kiss from Maddalena.* A recent Guggenheim fellow, Castellani is the artistic director of GrubStreet and is on the faculty of the MFA Program for Writers at Warren Wilson College. He lives in Boston.

The text of *The Art of Perspective* is set in Warnock Pro, a typeface designed by Robert Slimbach for Adobe Systems in 2000. Book design by Wendy Holdman. Composition by Bookmobile Design & Digital Publisher Services, Minneapolis, Minnesota. Manufactured by Versa Press on acid-free, 30 percent postconsumer wastepaper.